After Armageddon

By

Thomas D. "Thom" Cantrall

Prologue

Many millions of years ago disaster was headed towards an unaware and unwary world. This world was heavily populated with many diverse creatures large and small. Their world seemed to them to be stable and would endure forever, for had it not endured since the beginning of their memories? There was a hierarchy of sorts that ruled this world. It was a hierarchy of the strong and the wise and in a clash of those two, generally the strong will out for truly, in the world of the blind, is not the individual with one eye the king?

Such was life on this world until a fateful day when, from a clear and perfect sky fell a rock. There was nothing special or unusual about this rock except, perhaps, its larger size for had not rocks been falling from that same sky for as long as that world had existed? What made this rock so different was that in a short time nine species in ten on this heavily populated world would no longer exist!

We can assume that this rock was huge. This rock was the size of the largest mountain standing on our world today. Had man lived on this world at this time he would have seen a brilliant, burning light in the sky as the rock hurtled through the atmosphere of that world and was heated beyond white-hot by it. This spectacle would have been visible across much of this world and would have, no doubt, scared him catatonic... but not for long.

There was no man on that world at that time and there was no record written of it with pen and paper but, it happened. It is written in the rocks if not on paper on that world. When this giant mountain hurtled out of space, I'm sure that myriad eyes turned heavenward and watched it as it sped to his destiny at the edge of a great ocean where it struck with such force and power that we can only imagine it today from our safe distance and separation in time. When this rock struck, the explosion was greater than any human has ever seen. The fireball was so immense it immediately incinerated everything in a huge circle many miles across. These were probably the luckiest of its victims in this cursed world for the explosion ripped and pulverized billions of tons of the native soil and stone and sent a cloud of near flour consistency particles around the world, obliterating the sun and creating an unending night that would last beyond the lives of most of the population of this world.

Now, all at an instant, size and power mattered not a whit. The large and the powerful were destroyed as quickly and as readily as the weak and the timid. Around this world, the sun was not to be seen... it was winter with no plants growing.

The herbivores were starving now and with them went those who preyed on them. The giant and the intelligent and the stupid... the wise and the vapid... predator and prey... it mattered not how large, how mean, how strong or how well endowed... all were doomed. These creatures were not just some individuals but entire species all over this world were doomed It was not just a few species or some select species that were doomed, but virtually every species that lived on the surface of this ancient world were to disappear in the mere twinkling of a geological eye.

Only those species that could escape the surface of this now barren, cold and deserted planet had any chance of surviving.   Those that did not rely on the myriad surface species for food, shelter or survival had a chance.

One, a relatively small, previously unimportant family did survive.   This small creature about the size and shape of our shrew was able to outlast the years and years of interminable winter.   From this innocuous creature and others like him, life returned to the desolate world.   There were creatures that swam in the vast seas that survived this holocaust.   There may have even been some avian species that were able to live on, but the survivors were few and they were scattered widely as food was nowhere plentiful.

It was part of a plan... an infinite plan that some would survive and others who had prepared the way but were not destined to continue would not survive for their part was done and many millions of years later a new species would arrive on this world.   They were the first species with the ability to understand the nature of this plan and their part in it and they were to rule this world and have dominion over it even as they ruled over the flora and fauna thereon and had dominion over it... and God looked over the work of the sixth day and saw it was good...

Table of Contents

Chapter 1
The Mission

The sun was just rising over the crescent that was earth, creating a most spectacular aura as the shuttle approached the enormous monolith streaking through space. Tensions were high and the atmosphere charged with a strange brand of energy as the men thought about the task ahead of them.

Massive Asteroid in Space

In sight of their optics now, the asteroid loomed into view as the menace it was. Huge, lumbering and mindless, it charged on through the near earth space that meant danger. There was not a man aboard this shuttle that did not know in his heart that the chance of success in their mission was slight and the opportunity to die was high, but still they approached the deadly monolith with the tenacity of the Marines in the Mike Boats approaching Guadalcanal so many years ago. None knew what awaited them aside from stark terror, but all were as ready as man could make them to assault this foreign beach so far from home.

Their mission was simple: attach an explosive device in such an orientation as to effect a slight change of direction of the huge rock. At the distance they were from earth, it wouldn't take much, but the drone flights that had been attempted earlier had not been successful for a variety of reasons. Most prevalently, the charges had not been of sufficient magnitude to dislodge the asteroid from its orbit to any measurable degree. Those efforts had been under the auspices of the United Nations and, as such, the pacifists of the world ruled and nuclear devices were not employed in the effort. This expedition was different. It was not a United Nations mission, but was under the command and control of the North Atlantic Treaty Organization, NATO, and included all of Europe and Russia in the planning, timing and execution of the event.

It had taken time to refit and outfit the retired space

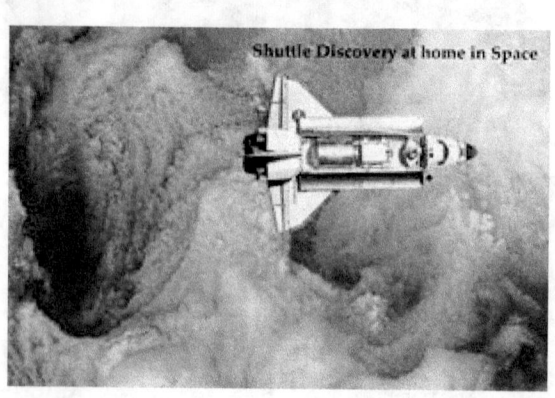
Shuttle Discovery at home in Space

shuttle, Discovery, for this mission. An entire new crew had to be assembled, trained and armed for the mission. Time was now the enemy. As it elapsed, it made the likelihood of success ever less likely. As the deadly menace closed the distance between itself and earth, the angle of deflection necessary to cause the giant to slide by safely increased significantly. "If we had used a nuclear device to nudge it when they first defined the danger," the pro-nuclear side had declared, "it would be a fait accomplii now and there would be no danger."

"You cannot prove that," the anti-nuclear people responded, "and the residual radiation may have dire consequences for us all. What good to save us from the asteroid only to doom us all to a permanent nuclear fallout that would eventually kill us all?"

Thus the arguments loomed though the months and years it took to build and utilize the drone craft that delivered too little payload from too far away and so necessitated this high risk evolution now underway. The costs to recommission the retired spacecraft were heavy, but were borne by the entire community involved. Even Japan had participated to a limited degree but one of those now seated in the shuttle as it neared its goal was Japanese. Hiro Yashita was a mathematical genius who had been recruited to aid the team in the proper placement of the explosive device. It was her calculations that told the powers that be that the ten mega-ton device they'd planned on using was insufficient and that the Russian fifty mega-ton device would be barely adequate for what they had planned.

"You cannot prove that," the anti-nuclear people responded, "and the residual radiation may have dire consequences for us all. What good to save us from the asteroid only to doom us all to a permanent nuclear fallout that would eventually kill us all?"

Thus the arguments loomed though the months and years it took to build and utilize the drone craft that delivered too little payload from too far away and so necessitated this high risk evolution now underway. The costs to recommission the retired spacecraft were heavy, but were borne by the entire community involved. Even Japan had participated to a limited degree but one of those now seated in the shuttle as it neared its goal was Japanese. Hiro Yashita was a mathematical genius who had been recruited to aid the team in the proper placement of the explosive device. It was her calculations that told the powers that be that the ten mega-ton device they'd planned on using was insufficient and that the Russian fifty mega-ton device would be barely adequate for what they had planned.

Approaching the rock had taken even more of the precious commodity. Now, as the task at hand was completed, Mission Commander, Air Force Colonel Robert Bruce, knew well, they were over budget on fuel usage and if they could not conserve fuel on their return burn, they would reach earth, alright, at approximately twenty-four thousand miles per hour and without sufficient fuel to slow themselves would either skip off into deep space, never to be seen again on earth, or would burn themselves to death as had Columbia when her heat shield failed on reentry on the first of February, 2003. In conversation with his on-board experts, it was decided that no one would know of this. It would do no good as there was no fueling station between them and home, so to worry the others would be needless. It was what it was, nothing more. Either he could coax a few extra kps out of the old girl while saving a few kilograms of fuel or they would not make it. There were no other options.

It seemed like the Extra-Vehicular Activity would never end as the French Astronaut, Guy DeMonde, and his team placed the explosive device at precisely the point indicated by Hiro Yashita. When Guy's team was finally done and Hiro was satisfied that everything was as perfect as it could be made, the word was passed to the command deck and Discovery began the slow turn that would point her in the direction of home. Colonel Bob exercised a gentle hand in firing the huge main engines for just a momentary burn... just enough to get them started in the correct trajectory. It was his firm belief and prayer that the earth's gravity would grab them as they got closer and would do for them what he had not the fuel to do from this far out. For this part of the journey, he would know in a matter of an hour or so if he had been successful. In the meantime he would simply ignore the entreaties from Houston as to why his burn was so much shorter than they had planned. What they didn't know wouldn't hurt them at this point and if his gambit were unsuccessful, it would matter not a whit to anyone on that shuttle either. It was at 1450:28 Zulu when Discovery, in optimal earth orbit once again fired to slow her forward speed in order to begin reentry... a reentry that was so close to being impossible as to not count at all. No one on board knew their plight save Colonel Bob alone and that was the way he wished it to be. The burn time necessary to generate sufficient negative Delta V was not known to him precisely. He had estimated it but it was the mega-computer in Houston Mission Control that told Discovery how long to apply the brakes. From this point on, he was merely a passenger like everyone else on board... Perhaps not precisely like everyone else for he knew what might be, they did not.

It was not lost on the Colonel that the insertion burn ended when the available fuel was

Discovery Touchdown

exhausted. He knew not whether it was enough. Houston

asked him on a tight line what had happened and he had told them, simply, "I'm out of gas… God ride with us now."

God did indeed ride with the crew that day for, though they were a bit hot, they had, indeed, had enough fuel to brake sufficiently to make their usual dead-stick landing.   After that insertion burn, main engine and maneuvering fuel was no longer necessary as the craft was in total free-fall mode and it was merely the laws of aerodynamics and gravity that controlled the remainder of the flight.   If effect, when the shuttle emerged from its reentry phase and the heat shields held, surface temperatures began to drop and Bob Bruce, Mission Commander and Air Force full bird Colonel knew that they had made it safely for now it he was merely piloting a glider, albeit a very large glider, into the dry lake bed that was Edwards Air Force Base in Southern California.

The actual touch down and landing was uneventful and clearly anticlimactic as the graceful Discovery approached the runway with her escort F-16's flying close support. The actual touch down occurred amid the cheers of thousands of onlookers and well-wishers. All knew there was something special afoot because of the publicity surrounding the refitting and launching of the retired craft. International media had learned there was an asteroid that was a thing of interest in near earth orbit, but no one knew exactly what the crew had achieved. That the rock was an imminent danger to earth was a well-kept secret by all the governments of earth who were in the know on this subject. The member nations of the UN had been told of the conventional explosive detonations by the unmanned drones and were subsequently told that this mission was to verify that sufficient movement had taken place to remove the threat from earth. No one knew otherwise.

Once the shuttle crew was safely back on earth and the crew of the International Space Station had been retrieved by the Russians with one of their large Soyuz space craft, the time had come to detonate the device left behind by the shuttle crew. That crew had been invited to join the Soyuz attackers made up the audience that relaxed and watched the countdown clock as it diminished inexorably towards it's 0600 Zulu (1500 PDT) zero point.

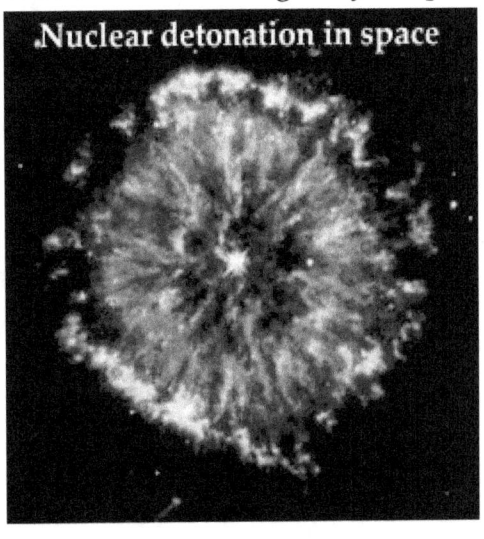
Nuclear detonation in space

Those who expected the typical mushroom cloud to appear at the instant of detonation were surprised to see not that, but what looked like a bright sphere of colors more brilliant than anything ever experienced on earth. Of course, there was no atmosphere where the detonation occurred nor was there any matter to be picked up and charged by the tremendous release of energy. These were things of earth, not of space. What occurred there was a pure release of energy in all directions universally and simultaneously. At the center of this nebula was a chunk of stone. Large, smooth, mostly iron and entirely dangerous, it resisted the forces amassed against it by the explosion for the most part.

All the experts had assumed, erroneously, that the rock was uniform in make-up and density. If that had been the case, it would most likely have been pushed violently out of its trajectory and would have continued its travels through space probably to be drawn into the intense gravity well of the sun were it would have been consumed like a gnat by a bird with no more ill effect than a slight burp by the sun as it swallowed its morsel. That was not the case. An amateur astronomer had tried to

Goldendale Observatory

convince the vaunted scientists that their theory of a uniform density and mass was not necessarily true in this case. This asteroid was enormous... almost a small planetoid and it was not spherical, it looked for all the world like an oversized Idaho Baker Potato. Vaughn Murray, who had originally brought the existence of this rock to the attention of the scientific community, thought he could detect an anomaly in it. He was an amateur, but he was not without experience. He had spent his career, all forty years of it working for a major aerospace contractor at the Goldendale, Washington Observatory. This was the same observatory so prominent in the proof of Einstein's Theory of Relativity. He was not an astronomer but a mathematician without a doctorate so his opinions were not sought after and, even more, were not paid much attention. What Mr. Murray had seen had convinced him that the asteroid was of two parts... one iron and the other part something else. He wasn't sure what that part was, but it did not appear to him to be uniform in density.

It was this anomaly of density that Mr. Murray had postulated that doomed the mission. With such a large disparity of densities in the mountain of stone, the detonation, while in the geographical center of the asteroid was not anywhere near the balance point of it. The result was that when the explosion occurred, the rock began to spin in a circle about the center point and continue its basic trajectory toward earth... and destiny.

Chapter II
The Argument

"I don't care what the social scientists say," shouted Senator Richard Kyle, R-ID. The people of the world deserve to know what is happening. Yes, I understand there is every chance that we may be missed by this object, but there is an even greater chance that in just three days' time life could cease to exist on our planet. People deserve to know this!"

"Now really, Senator, don't you think you're being just a bit melodramatic here," drawled Senator Clay Pyle D-MS. "I mean, I know the people of Idaho are probably more resourceful than those in the rest of the country, but do you really believe that, even if it hits, it will be all that bad? I mean, Senator... this is just a piece of rock... it's not a bomb or anything... what can it do to the earth?"

Senator Kyle sputtered in his impotence at the denseness of his colleague. "Senator Pyle, have you ever heard of the dinosaurs?"

"Now, Senator, don't be insulting. Of course I've heard of the dinosaurs. They lived on earth many thousands of years ago and are all gone now."

"And just how did they disappear? What happened to them? An asteroid hit Earth some sixty-five million years ago and wiped them out. An asteroid, I might point out, that is thought to have been smaller than the one

16

approaching us now," the Idaho Senator shouted, having lost his composure in the face of such obstinacy.

"Oh come now," Senator Pell retorted with a laugh, "that is a theory that is not even accepted by all of the scientific community. Everyone knows that dinosaurs lived before the flood and were wiped out in it. Since Noah lived no more than five or six thousand years ago,

LDS Meeting House

those dinosaurs could not have been killed off any millions of years ago. Anyone who understands the bible knows that the earth can be no older than twelve thousand years. There is simply no reason to be concerned by a chunk of rock falling from the air. They happen every night and I am still here! There is," he continued, "simply no reason to be alarmed and to scare the good people of the world as to this incident is ludicrous. I'll not hear of it and there is no way that my committee will vote to lift the gag order on this heretical information!"

---   ...   ---

It was a luscious Sunday afternoon as is seldom found in the desert of eastern Washington in December. The temperature was over fifty degrees and the bright sun shone at a low angle in the sky as the shortest day of the year approached. Christmas was the subject on nearly every lip as the congregation of the Columbia River Ward of the

17

Church of Jesus Christ of Latter-day Saints, the Mormons, dismissed from its three hour block of meetings. As is the wont of church brothers worldwide, there were small groups of men gathered to chat and catch up on events since they'd last had the opportunity to meet. Mothers were chasing down exuberant children and depositing the captives into the custody of smiling fathers and the discussion of one such group turned to the subject on one of the talks they'd heard this week before Christmas.

"Jared," asked a curious Adam Stuart, "what did you think of the talk on food storage today? Do you think there is significance to it due to the timing so near the Christmas Holiday? I know we need to do more along that line. Heavens, the Prophets have been admonishing us to do so for generations now, but what do you think?"

"Adam," Jared replied, "Janine and I have been doing our best to get that done. We've even devoted this Christmas to that end. We have a few small gifts for the children, but we've dedicated the rest of our Christmas budget to preparing our family for whatever might come. Two years ago, when I was out of work for those two months, our emergency supplies really helped sustain us and I don't ever want to be caught short. We're in pretty good shape right now and if you need help or advice, just let me know. We learned a lot about getting this done and we'd like to help others with what we've learned."

"That's a super offer, Jared. Tomorrow is Family Home Evening and I'd like to have a lesson on that for my family, as young as they are. Do you suppose you and Janine and the kids might come over and share a dinner with us and give that lesson? I know Mondays are not usually for that, but I feel a special urgency and I think this would help. Rae Lynn is a bit reluctant to spend anything on this right now with Christmas so close but I think it's necessary... perhaps we can discuss that as well?"

"I'll certainly have to clear it with Janine, but I think we can do just that. Since I'm your home teacher it's altogether fitting to do so. How about if we show up about six pm and we can go from there?"

Monday evening found the two couples and their children deep in discussion over the concept, the rationale and the mechanics of storing a year's worth of goods against need. Jared explained to the young couple that it had, indeed been a principle of the Church that each family should keep on hand everything that would be needed to sustain that family for the next year in case of extreme need. He went on to explain how his family had accomplished their goal in this area and illustrated how other families in the congregation had done so as well. Jared explained that there was an emergency planning specialist in their ward and that he was available at any time to help out with their plan.

When alone again that night, Adam and Rae Lynn talked late into the night about the subject. Rae wanted to know why Adam was feeling such a strong need now to do this.

"I'm not sure what is prompting it. I know I've been watching that television show "Doomsday Preppers" and that has got me thinking. Oh, I know that so many of those people are preparing for something that may well never occur, but the underlying tenet is true… we must be prepared to help ourselves if the need ever arises. And, we certainly know that losing a job is a real possibility. It was as Jared said; their storage saved their house when he was out of work for so long when his company went bankrupt in this lousy economy. It left him with nowhere to turn except to himself. If they'd had to put out money on groceries and clothing for that period, they could not have met their monetary obligations and they could well have had serious difficulties."

"It does make sense, Honey," the pretty blonde said, "but what about Christmas? I know our kids are not old enough to really understand what it's all about, but I do want to start our traditions early."

"I totally agree with that, Baby," he answered, "but what tradition is most important? I mean our children will be very happy with a couple of new toys and some bright, new clothes and the boxes they came in. You and I understand the rationale and can limit our expense for the good of our family. What say you?"

With a sigh, Rae Lynn said, "I have to agree, now is the time to do it. We've been saving all year so we would not have any debt from our Christmas, so why don't we be very frugal with gifts for the kids and use that money to lay in what we need and call that the greatest family gift ever?"

With the decision made, Adam and Rae spent Tuesday evening, December 18th buying the staples any family would need to sustain themselves. It was not a year's worth, but it was a start… a very good start, they admitted and by the time Wednesday was done, it was all carefully stored in their ample basement along with four fifty-five gallon drums of fresh water treated with just a drop or two of chlorine bleach each to retard bacterial growth and to retain its freshness and purity. On Wednesday night, Adam and Rae Lynn went to bed with a sense of calm and self-satisfaction they'd never known in their lives. There was food in storage. There was water available. There was even fuel for all their camping appliances. Not enough yet, but some... and more to come.

---   ...   ---

It was not until Wednesday evening, December 19th that the President went on National Television to explain to the American people what was coming. While the world eavesdropped, the President calmly explained that, while a large asteroid was rapidly approaching Earth, it was still unclear if it would actually hit us and even if it did, he had been assured that the damage would be confined to the local area. In the unlikely event of a North American landing, FEMA and Homeland Security stood poised to help out immediately. It was felt that since the earth was some four-fifths water, the chances were high that it would simply collide with the ocean and, although a tsunami could result, the aftermath could be easily controlled. He went on to urge caution and care in the next few days and warned that any acts of looting or anyone taking advantage of the situation would be severely dealt with by agencies of the Federal Government as well as by state and local authorities. He signed off with a cheery wave and a wish for a happy winter holiday season and a prosperous New Year.

21

Chapter III
Impact

The eastern sky was beginning to show light but the sun had not yet made its appearance when Steve Warren, a member of the same Columbia River Ward as Jared and Adam, saw a beyond bright streak across the early morning sky. It lit the sky like midday and left a distinct after image in the northern sky. It took but a moment for him to realize what he'd seen and he immediately called his family from their sleep to assemble in the basement. From there he began calling the people on his phone tree... a system set up within the ward where all members could be quickly notified in case of an emergency. This he considered a huge emergency. Neither he nor any member he had talked to believed a word of the President's assurances from the evening before and they had all made a pact to initiate the emergency calling tree if something actually happened. This streak was definitely a "something".

Asteroid Impact

Of course, there were ward members who had family and friends in adjacent wards so they called them as well. The result was, over ninety percent of the Church membership in this eastern Washington community knew what had been forecast had occurred. It is a sign of the efficiency of personal preparedness that so many people were awakened in time to gather to the relative safety of basements and storm cellars throughout the three cities. It is estimated that twenty percent of the one-hundred and fifty thousand residents of the Tri-City area are members of this church. Of course there were others in the area that received warning and made their way to the nether regions of their homes. Those in apartments had no such retreat but even they had a plan... a plan which they now implemented.

No one knew how long it would be before the blast would reach them and they waited... Huddled in close places families joined in prayer that they might be saved from the sure holocaust to follow. All knew disaster was coming; none knew when or how severe it would be. When it came, it came as a surprise. Oh, probably not so much a surprise in fact as a surprise in intensity.

No one knew where the great, twelve mile long rock actually struck the ground. Perhaps they would never

Devastated Timber

know. What they did know, however was that the impact was tremendous. Very early on the people in this community felt a huge, pressing force that seemed to tear the very breath from their bodies. First came the sonic boom associated with any object moving through the atmosphere at greater than the speed of sound. The force of this shock wave broke virtually every piece of exposed glass in the region. The sound was deafening... like the sound of a battery of sixteen inch guns on the battleship USS Missouri being fired simultaneously. Ear drums were broken by this great blast and structures were flattened. Even substantially built homes and buildings suffered severe damage from this shock wave. Unfortunately, the shock wave was just the beginning of the destruction.

In such cases, the sonic shock wave creates a single, short duration stress on all that it touches. The effect on rigid or semi-rigid structures can be intense, resulting in enormous and catastrophic failures. More often, however, this shock wave is but the precursor what is to come. Such was the case this early December morning. Upon striking earth, no matter where it struck, a tremendous explosion occurred. In this case, with a meteor more than twelve miles long and five miles wide, that explosion was beyond the force of a million Hiroshima sized Atom Bombs. A mushroom cloud rose so high that it reached the stratosphere. The clouds hid the next danger from the impact. From the epicenter, spreading out like the rings in a pond from a stone, a tremendous pressure wave circumnavigated the entire globe. Everywhere, with no real haven, the massive wave flattened what the prior sonic wave merely rattled. This huge overpressure sped on like a rocket sled on rails without mind or reason; following only one prime directive... it was an area of high pressure, so it sought an area of lower pressure. As elevated at the pressure was in the circulating wave, the entire earth was lower in pressure than it so it raced around the world spreading death and destruction.

This wave of destruction was horrific around the entire world. Everywhere, structures were leveled. Of course, individual homes had no chance to withstand this chaos and were either flattened or simply blown away. Larger structures like low-rise, multi-story buildings fared little better and most were destroyed. Even the largest and most solidly constructed edifices were damaged heavily and the loss of life was horrendous. Millions died instantly and millions more were injured so badly that their fate was sealed. If the destruction had ended here, Earth would have lost over fifty percent of her population of humans, and nearly all large animals... but it didn't stop here.

The huge overpressure wave surged outward from the impact point and did its best to implode all it touched. It exerted tremendous crushing forces on everything it touched, but for sheer destruction, its effects were miniscule as compared to what was to follow. Immediately after the passing of the forceful pressure wave, there came another wave... of underpressure. Where the initial wave had tried to squeeze everything it touched into as small a package as it could... somewhat like squeezing a rubber ball in one's hand, this underpressure wave, an area of intense low pressure caused all that still being squeeze to now expand rapidly to attempt to fill the void it created naturally. Structures that resisted the push of the Overpressure wave now found themselves assaulted by a force that few were designed to resist... a force that wanted them to EXPLODE outward. Immediately, any glass not destroyed by the prior pressure wave was now totally demolished by this great suction. Entire skyscrapers were exploded such that there was nothing remaining but, perhaps, the ribs of steel that formed the outline of the structure. Destruction was complete now. Around the world, so little remained living that the yet to come firestorm was almost an anticlimax.

The world had ceased to exist on this late December day for all intents and purposes. Why one building remained standing while entire blocks were flattened around it, no one knew. But it happened. Rome, with its seven hills, was as it was when Romulus and Remus first laid eyes on it. Nothing stood. Most of Europe fared poorly because of

Cretaceous Period

the antiquity of its building. Asia died a fiery death. North and South America were not to be recognized... had anyone been there to try. It was as it had been sixty-five million years prior when a similar, though smaller asteroid struck the Yucatan Peninsula of Mexico and over ninety percent of all species living perished in the same scenario as had just occurred on this pre-Christmas day in December, 2012. The dinosaurs were gone for these millions of years... now it seemed man was too.

Chapter IV
After

It had been totally silent for nearly thirty hours when Jared Stone dared to think about emerging from his cocoon to see what remained. He did not hold much hope for anything of value remaining. His family had cuddled closely in their bomb-shelter type basement and listened in sheer fright as the events of the day transpired. The waiting was, by far the hardest part. That there would be great destruction, they knew well for the sounds of their home being crushed and destroyed was loud in their hearing. Like bombs exploding, they heard the fate befall their neighbors. The cul-de-sac on which they lived was made up of twelve single and split level, wood frame homes... the typical home for the middle class in this middle class community. Jared and Janine had lived in this home since they had relocated to this desert community some eleven years prior to take a position with Battelle Northwest's "Pacific Northwest National Laboratory" on the Hanford Nuclear Reservation nearby. The young family had lived here among friends for the entire time since. Of the eleven homes on this street, nine of them were owned by members of their same church. Now, he wondered if any of those friends had survived.

Over the protestations of Janine, Jared tested the exit door, finding it only partially blocked by the debris that was once their home. With care and with no small amount of trepidation, he worked his way out of the confines and relative safety of his bunker like basement. As he emerged into the gloom of a dismal December afternoon, the man stopped and stared. The scene that greeted him was something he'd have only expected to see in the aftermath of a nuclear attack. As far as he could see, there was nothing left intact. Not a single tree stood in a housing development old enough to have grown its trees to a mature status. Where yesterday there had been the plane trees, birches and others that had afforded a summer's shade today there was nothing. Not a single building stood. Nowhere within his range of vision was there anything that even suggested that this had so recently been a vibrant, living community. Here and there lay a pile of smoking lumber... the remains of a family's home. Nowhere was there life or any sign of it. No children played in mowed yards. No pets stalked imaginary interlopers. No birds sang from leafed trees or flowering shrub. It was as if life had moved away from this Kennewick Park neighborhood.

Jared let his gaze rise to the heavens... perhaps in supplication, but more likely in grief at what he was seeing. While it was not uncommon for December days to be overcast, what he saw here was beyond that. The sky seemed to be a living thing with a maelstrom of roiling clouds dominating the scene. Silently, the man watched the boiling cauldron above him and wondered for sure, "What hath God wrought?" Never in his existence and, he was sure, in the term of his parents or even his grandparents had such a scene presented itself. He knew he must be looking at what Hiroshima and Nagasaki looked like on the morning after the blasts that destroyed them. But, this was bigger, he was sure. Those were, in each case, a single city destroyed by a single bomb. This, he reasoned, had to cover thousands of miles. It was not reasonable to think that he was in the epicenter of the blast. The odds were simply too high for that to be possible. That meant that this destruction had to cover more area than those early atomic blasts ever could have done.

As Jared looked across the desolation that had, just hours before, been a living, vibrant city of nearly eighty thousand people in a greater metropolitan area of over a quarter of a million people. He wondered now if any of those were still living. There had to be, he reasoned, some like he and his family, who had burrowed into prepared spaces and had come through this disaster but how to contact them? They couldn't all be dead, could they? He mused silently. As he gazed across the now barren landscape, his mind began working feverishly.

It is reasonable that some survived as I did. It is also reasonable that without help, no one would be alive in ninety days. There was no food left in this land save what was in a storage area such as my own. There was no transportation of any kind for any price. In fact, "price" had just become an archaic term. First, he decided, we must see what happened in our own area and he moved out slowly.

Down the street he moved to the house he'd visited just this past Monday. He found the ruins of the Stuart home and began probing through what detritus remained. It was the work of but a few minutes to locate the remains of the stairway leading down into the basement of the house. When he finally cleared enough of an access to actually reach the door, a chore made extremely difficult by the remains of a refrigerator and a kitchen range that had lodged into the narrow passage that led directly into the subterranean storage area, creating a nearly impenetrable barrier to the area. When he rapped sharply on the door, he was rewarded with a quick response.

"Who is there?" a very scared woman's voice rang out. "Who is it? I've tried to get out and I can't open the door."

"It's Jared," the man replied and I've cleared the passage, unlock it and try again. I think it's open now."

"Oh my, Jared, I'm so happy to see you!" The girl shouted as she pushed the door open as wide as she could. Adam is hurt and I think Jenny is dead. We had a wall collapse and they were caught in the falling material... I couldn't get to them and I haven't heard either for some hours now."

"Take the baby and go to my house," Jared stated firmly. "Watch our kids and send Janine to me at once. She is a nurse and she will know what to do. Do you have water here? Also, do you have medical supplies?"

"We do," the young mother stated, "but I can't leave Adam and Jenny. I don't know what's wrong and they may need me."

"They need medical help more right now," the man stated strongly. "Go do as I say and I will do what I can here. Janine can help me and we will call for you as soon as we can."

With that, the scared woman retreated from the ruins that had been her home and made her way with young Adam Junior, AJ to everyone, to the site of Jared's ruined home. It was but a moment or two before Janine arrived and she and her husband set in on the task of clearing the collapsed wall enough to find the missing.

In the course of this task, the couple spoke but little and concentrated on clearing debris. On they pressed, until, at last, they could see the way through to the small side room where the accident had occurred. Immediately on entering the room, Janine found three year old Jenny unconscious beneath a collapsed set of shelves. It was the work of but mere moments to determine that the youngster still breathed though it was shallow and thready. That she was in shock was evident so the first course was to treat the shock and then explore for further injury. When Janine Stone had completed her cursory exam and found no further trauma, she determined to move the tiny one

At a loss

out of further danger and to get her to a place where she could be better treated and more thoroughly examined.

"Jared," the nurse said, "we need a litter of some type to carry Jenny to our house. Have you found any sign of Adam yet?"

"Yes, baby," the man replied. "I have him located and I'm trying to clear the stuff out of the way to get to him. He's still but I can see him breathing. Should we move her now and come back for Adam, or should we wait until I can get him out?"

"Is the spot he's in stable or is there danger of more falling on him?" she asked.

"I think he's safe enough. He's in a little cave formed by some shelving and a couple of timbers. It looks pretty solid for now."

"OK," she said. "Let's get the baby to her mother. Rae Lynn is beside herself with worry, I'm sure and having Jenny with her may well help her calm down."

It took but a minute to find the makings for a serviceable litter and the two neighbors carried the little girl back to her mother. On arriving, they had to calm the woman and convince her that Jenny was merely out, not dead but the nurse, Janine, explained what the woman should do and that shock was the most dangerous thing to combat now. While talking with the distraught mother, Janine had taken the opportunity to perform a more detailed exam and found that, indeed, there seemed to be no great injury to the girl.

While the couple was preparing to return to the demolished home, their oldest daughter, Rachel came forth and asked if she could join them and help. It was but a moment's pause before Janine hugged her daughter and said, "Of course you may, Darling. I know how resourceful you are and you have studied first aid and helped me before, so, yes, I'd welcome your help."

Twenty minutes later Adam Stuart was free of his trap and was stirring awake. His left arm was obviously broken but it was not a compound fracture and the two Stone healers had made it immobile while they prepared him for transport back to their own area. Jared had found a wooden door to which he had affixed to long studs he had salvaged creating a very serviceable litter on which to transport the injured man. As soon as he had completed this task, he left his women to their tasks and moved to the next house in the hopes of finding more survivors. He explained to Janine that he was going to do a quick survey of their block and see if he could find more people.

Nodding, she sent him on his way telling him that they would sit with Adam in hopes that he would regain consciousness and perhaps they wouldn't have to carry him back home. "After all," she explained, "if he can walk, even with help, it would be simpler than Rachel and me trying to carry him."

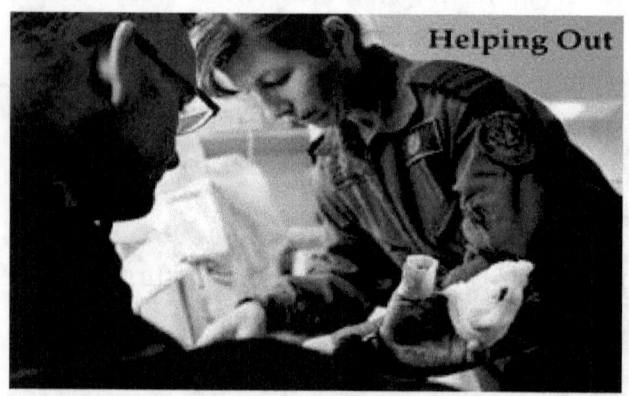
Helping Out

At the first home, the one next to the Stuarts, there was no life. They had evidently not received warning and were simply not around. The second house yielded a very healthy couple with two strong but shaken teen-age boys and a very pretty seventeen year old young woman. It took but a moment to urge them out and explain what was being done in the neighborhood. The family immediately volunteered to take over the search so Jared could get back to his family and the injured Adam. Reluctantly, Jared acquiesced and hurried back to find Janine and Rachel supporting a very unsteady, but equally determined Adam in the vertical position. When Jared replaced his daughter the chore became easier and the little convoy made their way back to the remains of the Stone's home.

By evening, all of the homes on their little cul-de-sac had been searched and of the eleven, plus the one across the cross street, homes there, people were found alive, in various conditions of health and well-being in but five of them. In all cases, these homes did not have a full basement and/or the families had had no prior warning. Deceased persons were found in two of the homes and in those homes where people were found alive, there were casualties. In all, of the sixty-eight people who resided on the street prior to the meteor impact, only twenty four were still alive and of those, five were in very critical condition. Their injuries were beyond the capabilities of the one nurse available and medical supplies were extremely limited.

The six able bodied men and women sat in a small circle late in the day and considered what to do next. First, they decided, a shelter would be needed and it was determined that for tonight, at least, a lean-to of sorts would be built from the copious quantities of waste lumber that and so recently been part of the houses in the area. The fact that other neighborhoods would be doing the same as they had just done and would probably be having similar results was discussed and agreed upon. It was understood that not all those who survived would have a desire to cooperate with other survivors to make conditions better for all and that protection would be imperative. The final outcome of this impromptu lesson in pure democracy was a decision to fort up here for tonight with an armed watch set over the group. Tomorrow, a patrol would go out to make contact with similar groups in the area with an idea of finding a better preserved structure to house the group. Also on the search list was a doctor. For those injured, this was a high priority. Without medical help, the fate of these people was far from certain...

Daylight came late Christmas morning and found a small group of people huddled around a fire wondering if they were the only people left in the world. Like Jared's group, they had dug themselves out of the remains of their homes and had banded together for mutual support and interest. This group was in a formerly quiet neighborhood of the alphabet house community of Richland. Also like Jared's group, they were predominately members of the LDS church as, it seems, this was the group that had gotten the word of the danger passed to its members in time that they could, often, shelter in place adequately to save some lives. To be sure, even near each other. One was on its side and required a huge community effort using found ropes, blocks and sheaves to set it upright. That it would never move again was obvious, but with the help of some appropriated hand tools, a set of serviceable steps was made to access each of them and they then began to serve as the headquarters for the Bomber Camp (named for the high school team, Richland Bombers) of meteor survivors. They were few in numbers, but dedicated to survival.

One important addition to this group occurred when Bart Roberts was brought in with his wife and fourteen year old daughter. Bart had been a ham radio operator all his life and while he didn't have power to operate his earth link station as he had before the impact, he did have portable, hand held, battery powered FM radios that he volunteered for the group. It was Bart's radios, in fact, that first told the Bomber Camp that there were other survivors in other areas. The former US Navy radioman had just installed his fifty watt base station in one of the converted railcars, strung a rudimentary antenna and powered it with the direct current from a battery scrounged from a wrecked car, of which there were many in easy reach when he heard an SOS call coming in, he determined, from the north towards the small town of Benton City. Although he could not directly help the caller, he was able to give him some general advice for his plight and to assure him that there were people still alive. It didn't take long for Bart to realize that this person was more afraid that he was alone in the world than he was of being killed now. The fellow had not seen another soul for the entire time since the impact and was quite sure this was the case. He was in a situation where he had sufficient food for a couple more days at least but was getting critical on water.

All over the area that had been the Tri-Cities, small bands of survivors came together for mutual support. These bands ranged from as few as three people to as many as thirty-five to forty. Most had a bit of food stored, but many did not and this created a problem. Initially, the sentiment among the groups was to share what they had, as they felt that help must surely be on the way. It was a matter of a week or so before it became apparent that there was not help to be had. An improved radio net had shown a similar situation to exist in all areas contacted. The large cities like Seattle and Portland seemed to be virtually depopulated.

There were only the scantest reports of survivors in the core areas and the high rise buildings were no more. In addition, gangs of outlaws roamed the area stealing what they wanted and murdering people with impunity. It was the tales of these gangs that caused the camps around the Tri-Cities area to come together in a meeting.

It was just past noon on a typically gloomy day with a light snow shower predominating when nearly one-hundred people began an in depth discussion of where to go from today. Surprisingly, one of the lowliest of structures had survived the best and, due to the fact that this area had been a major supplier of French fries to the McDonald's chain, there were several of these low, domed Quonset hut type of structures around. At this late time of the year, most of the fresh potatoes had been shipped, but there were still several sheds full of spuds yet to be processed. The huts made an adequate shelter and several had been repurposed to serve as dwelling places for the displaced families. Separate apartments had been partitioned into the nearly three thousand square feet of open space of the building and each family could get as fancy or as mundane as their time and resourcefulness allowed. It was at one of these spud sheds in a group of four such that served as the meeting place for the assembled group. A fire had been lighted in a center pit built for the purpose and it

Inside the Spud Shed

provided the heat and light necessary to make the meeting comfortable.

Since the meeting was held in the Kennewick Park Camp, Jared Stone presided and opened the meeting with a position statement that included the need for mutual protection of themselves and their supplies. The group organized themselves, initially, into a committee of the whole so they could then create such committees as were needed to address the concerns enumerated. Committees were formed to address such topics as food supplies and water resources. Others addressed protection and security. Transportation was a major concern and a new topic was public health.

Conducting the Meeting

Janine Stone chaired the Public Health Committee and Rae Lynn Stuart Chaired the Sub-Committee on available food in food storage under the umbrella of the Food Committee as was the Water Resources Sub-Committee specifically. Bart Roberts was brought is as the Chair for the Communications Committee and former Army Ranger and retired Colonel Andy Kline was ticketed for the Security and Protections Committee. The Transportation Committee was under the Chairmanship of Glenda Sykes, former manager of the Kennewick School District Bus System.

As the various committees were separated and the chairs selected their vice chairs and then broke into individual groups to discuss who would help in each area, a shout came from outside the door demanding admittance.

As this was not a closed meeting by any means, the small group demanding to be heard was ushered into the center of the group and asked what their concerns were.

Maya Jenson stepped to the fore as the spokesperson for the eight people assembled and in a quite belligerent tone began, "We were shut out of this meeting and we don't like that. We have every right to be part of whatever is decided." As she spoke, a murmur issued froth from them. "Maya," Jared began calmly, though he was quite tired of her obstructionist attitude, "We are only meeting to decide what committees need to be established. The people in this meeting are those who have experience in conducting such social experiments. As soon as the committees are named, we will be coming to the entire community for approval and for staffing of these committees. That is all that is happening here."

"I don't believe you," the woman persisted. "You are planning something behind our backs and we won't have that. We know our rights and you're violating them."

"Maya, let me explain something to you," intoned Julie Armistad, the only member of the legal community who had survived and had been found. "The only 'rights' any of us have are those granted within the community of which we are a part. There is no United States of America any longer. There is no Congress, no President and no Supreme Court. We are a small band of survivors of the worst calamity, I suspect, to hit the planet in sixty-five million years. As such, WE are the law! We are the judge, the jury and the executioner, as it were. No one has suggested anything that would justify this outburst of yours, so I would suggest you back out of here now and let us finish our work here so it can be presented to you later."

The woman spluttered and fumed in her indignation as she tried to shout down those who were called forth to remove her from the meeting. Her companions were a bit embarrassed, it seemed, by her antics and merely moved to the door to await what was to come.

When the Committee of the Whole had voted to adjourn to the general meeting and to explain what was done here, they moved as a group to the open area where all who wished could attend. As the group was called to order, Maya Jenson elbowed her way to the front of the crowd. There were several who would have protested, but a wave and a shake of the head from the dais told them that this was expected, so they held their silence and just tolerated the woman. As the meeting opened, Maya spoke up demanding to know who had appointed them the kings in this court.

Jared looked at the woman and began slowly... "Maya, how much food have you brought into the group?"

"That has nothing to do with it," she yelled. "I am a person and I don't need food to have the right to be heard."

Jared cut off further debate with her by asking, "Maya, how much water have you provided the group?" When she would have continued with her tirade, Jared simply said, "Maya you have contributed nothing. And the Committee of the Whole was made of up those who have contributed heavily in the necessities. We who have done so invited others who had specific skills to impart to the group. Do you have any special skills we need know about?"

Since it was well known that she was a high school dropout who worked as a clerk in a tanning spa, Jared had known the answer to that question as well. When she started to protest again, Jared, as the chair, simply stated that she had the choice to either sit quietly and follow the process or to be removed as before. In protest, she was seated though still muttering under her breath about the terrible way people were treated around here.

The various committees were presented and discussed by the population as a whole before a ratifying vote was taken on each body. The chair of that committee then made a statement as to his goals for his committee and they moved to the next. In this manner, a kind of new government was born here. Although it was not perfect, it did address the needs of the people at this time in this place in this circumstance.

All went quite smoothly until the Committee for Protection and Security was announced. It was at this point that Maya gained an ally. "Really, people, Marsha Johnston shouted, I cannot believe you! We have no need for this. We are  sane and reasonable people and I see no reason for guns in any form!"

When several people mentioned the presence of gangs in the area, she simply dismissed that with a wave. "These are sane, reasonable people. If we talk to them rather than try to shoot them, they will understand we want no trouble with them and they will simply go away!"

All protests to the contrary, notwithstanding, the woman never wavered from her stance and was appalled when her viewpoint was voted down so heavily. "We shall never carry guns," she stated and she, her husband and their two young adult children left the meeting in indignation.

That is your prerogative, of course, Mrs. Johnston," Colonel Kline stated, but I would like to know if those called on to protect you would be permitted the luxury?" Unfortunately, he never received an answer as the family was not out of range of his voice. "Damn fools," he muttered softly to no one in particular.

Colt AR 15

When the day's work was done and the committees were established, staffed and working, Colonel Kline called his committee together and they took inventory of all they had. It was at this time the colonel let his committee know they had a substantial arsenal of weapons at their disposal. As he was telling his people about the large number of AR 15's and other semi-automatic weapons they had accumulated by searching through destroyed homes and stores, looking for the gun safes that the blast had not been successful in destroying, a shout rang out from one of his lookouts. "Colonel, there are people on the hill. They are armed and they are coming this way!"

Chapter V
Them

Mud was falling from the sky and the earth looked like a huge gray slimeball when Juan and his brother Jose crawled from the ruins of their clubhouse. The two were smeared with the glop that was falling in waves from a gray, ash-laden sky. They did not know what had happened other than that something had exploded their world and the gang they had been a part of was no more. Of the twenty brothers  **Endless Ash** in that clubhouse, there were only two left alive. Juan had assumed the police had attacked them until he saw the gray gunk falling like some weird kind of snow. Jose was not so coherent. He was quite high on the meth the gang and finished cooking and nothing made a lot of sense to him just then. He was sure the lab had exploded and his mind was not working beyond that. It was true that their lab hadn't been the most attractive in town, but they had made thousands of dollars from its output.

As the brothers crawled away from the shambles of what was left of their center, Juan's mind began to clear and he worked hard to keep his brother focused. "Come on, 'mano," he snarled, "we have to get away from here. The police are going to be looking for what caused that explosion and I don't want to be anyplace near it when they show up. Don't worry about those left, they ain't going nowhere!

At Jose's dumbfounded look, Juan explained, "they all dead, bro. We be all that's left of this gang. I don't know what hit us, but something bad has happened. Look around us! There's junk falling from the sky and ever'thin'. Looks like a volcano blew up or something."

When Juan found a small shed still standing, he dragged his brother into it and pulled the door shut. He knew he had to get Jose straight again if they were going to be able to get out of this. He told his brother to sleep for a bit and as soon as his eyes shut, Juan slipped out into the gloom again to see what he could find. He knew enough to realize that food and water would be critical beyond all reason so he crossed the three blocks of destroyed buildings to reach the Safeway store at the Highlands... only there was no Safeway store there... in fact, there was nothing there but some detritus and a couple of badly wrecked cars. Locating the position of the store, the young Latino began digging through the rubble that remained. He was not seeking injured people; he was looking for food... any food and for water. The young man had lived long enough in Mexico to know that the water supply was not to be trusted. He was sure it would be contaminated with this falling stuff and would probably be poison.

His searching yielded some water bottles and a few beers and little else. It was the work of over two hours to locate enough food for the two young men for the rest of the day and he was worried about what would come next. There appeared to be not a single car anywhere that was operable. He was a master car thief and could have any car running in a matter of seconds... except there were none! The only vehicles to be seen were broken, bent and badly damaged hulks that, even if they could have been started, would not have been drivable.

With his bounty, Juan retreated to the small shack where he'd left his brother sleeping. He was concerned that Jose might have awakened and missed him, but, as it was, he need not have worried for the younger man was still snoring loudly when he entered this hole. It took several shakes to get the lad stirring and it was only after he told him he had bread and drink that the young man stirred and eventually came awake.

In the days that followed, the two brothers were afraid that they may be the only people left alive. They had seen no one and the sky continued to boil with fury as the Cascade Range volcanoes issued forth with mountains of ash and fumes. Although these people didn't know it at this time, the impact had caused a major shift in the tectonic plates around the Ring of Fire. Volcanoes were erupting from Tierra Del Fuego in far South America to the northern lands of Alaska. The eruptions extended down the Pacific Ocean all the way to Southeast Asia. The entire Ring of Fire was alive and in eruption, filling the skies with tons upon tons of ash and pumice.

It was over a week before the brothers found their first living soul. Even dead bodies were scarce and when found, they were often in the most grotesque poses.

Instinctively, the brothers knew to stay away from these victims. The sights only reinforced their fear of the water they found at different places. The girl they found was shaken and dirty, but did not appear to be hurt. She was not Latina and she spoke no Spanish and little English, but they could communicate well enough for her to understand that she was now part of their band. Although she didn't fully understand what this meant at this time, her upbringing in her native Chechnya had taught her that her protection… even her life was now in  the hands of these two young men. She had not eaten for several days and the bit of bread they gave her was a treat that she was more than willing to pay for in the only way, the only currency she owned. What had been two boys alone was now three and was soon to grow again.

Cruz Azul 13 they called themselves, after the Mexican professional soccer team and the Mexican Mafia with whom they had been, prior to the devastation, in a  want-to-be affiliation. As such, they were a tough pair. The addition of the female may have presented a problem to most pairs of males, especially brothers but these two had no problem sharing benefits so Ilya seemed to fit right in and together they continued to search for survival.

It was late in the day and food had been scarce and water even more so when the Cruz Azul 13 crew came on a ruined home that still had one wall standing. There were no bodies to be found but all three suspected that there had been people here recently. While they searched around the perimeter of the large home, they suddenly heard a moan from beneath a sheet of T-111 sheeting that drew them forward. As Juan moved to the sheet of plywood, Jose held a handgun they had scrounged from a ruined home a couple of days prior on the source of the sounds. Soundlessly the brothers moved into position and were on high alert as Juan lifted the sheet and flipped it away. What greeted them was a shirtless young man nearly buried in the soaking mud of ash that laid everywhere in this area.

"Help me," a voice croaked from the obviously injured young man. "Please help me," he groaned as he tried to lift himself to one elbow. As Jose raised his handgun to take careful aim at the distressed man, the older brother stopped him.

"Let's see what he's got, Bro," the young man said.

"We can do that a lot safer with him dead," Jose answered with a snarl.

"We can do that anytime," Ilya said. "He might now where some food is. We need that now, don't we?"

Rob

"That we do, girl," Juan said with a grin. "Come up outta that pit," he said to the man. I'm Juan. This is my bro, Jose and our woman Ilya. Who you be?"

48

After accepting some help getting to his feet and then to a place he could sit and rest a bit, he said calmly. "My name is Rob Kane and I was digging for some grits when that crap fell on me. My woman is here somewhere too." He let his eyes drift to the big pistol in the hands of the younger man and looked him in the eye, saying: "You can put that thing away. I'm no danger to you and I know where there's a good cache of food, but you use that and you'll never know about it."

When Kane had rested a bit and felt better, he began searching for his woman in the ruins he had so recently been buried beneath. Soon, the other men moved to help him but it was the woman Ilya that found her. At first the assembled rescuers thought the girl was unconscious but as the light hit her square in the face, she blinked and raised her hands to defend herself from the falling ash as the men moved to lift her from her trap. Surprisingly, she was not injured and was not really even that dirty, considering how badly used Rob had been.  Calmly she retrieved the sling like bag she had left on the ground where she had lain and replaced it around her neck and shoulders.

Shar rose from the ground and moved to Rob and asked what he needed. The young man just grinned at her and turned back to the brothers. "I'm ok now," he answered her. "But," he continued, "I have no idea what's coming down."

The rather large girl slid her hand into her bag and retrieved a very short, double-barreled shotgun and casually pointed it toward Jose and his now wholly inadequate handgun. "Baby," she intoned, "ain't nothing coming down 'round here but what we say is coming down..."

Rob grinned a slight grin and turned back to the brothers. "As I was saying, I know where there's food and water stored in plenty. If you want to help get it, we can eat good for quite a while but it's not gonna be easy. I've run onto a couple of gangs like yours before now and mostly they didn't survive. There's some hard cases running around now... bad boys who are just as big and bad as they want to be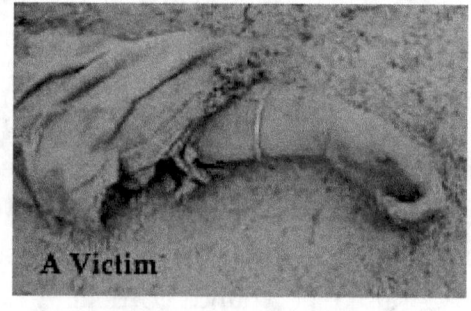

A Victim

until they run into someone that is bigger or badder. It's becoming a jungle here. There are only a few people around, but it seems they are all pretty bad."

Over the next hour or so, the five outcasts devised a plan of action that would, hopefully keep them alive in this land of the dead. Everywhere they went there was nothing but destruction and decay. Bodies were scarce, but not unheard of and daily, it seemed, another was found. There were very few people living. Once, in the distance, a group was seen moving through the rubble of a large structure but the CA-13 gang would not approach them. The gang was strong enough and certainly well enough armed as they had been finding and keeping a stash of weapons as they scavenged through the massive destruction. Although fear

50

did not figure into the equation, prudence did and since there was no real need to force the issue, they did not.

As time passed, others were added to the gang until they numbered about fourteen. Strangely enough in this social structure, the two first women emerged as the co-leaders of the group. Ilya and Shar were both intelligent and resourceful women who knew how to control the men of the group. That they were in demand, they knew and they used this to their advantage, bestowing their favors where it did them the most good. The two teamed up to run this group to their advantage. Fortunately, their advantage meant survival for the group and when they benefited, the entire group benefited.

Eventually, their group expanded to number ten men and four women. The men allowed to join them were strong and physical, but had to accept the rule as it was constituted. A few did not and were left behind. When one, a young

Jane Doe

Bosnian man who had definite ideas about who should be leading the group confronted Shar about her role, she simply slid the short-barreled bad gun from her sling bag and blew him completely out of his shoes. He had been accounted as one bad dude to this point, but on that day, the gang learned what bad really was.

The red haired girl, Jane, was added strictly as a tool. She didn't speak and was totally useless except for the most mundane of tasks, but with as many men as the group had, she had her uses and she had no need for speech to effect the chores she was set to accomplish. No one knew her name and she wouldn't or couldn't say, so she was simply Jane Doe. The other woman, Sara, was more communicative than Jane, but was not prone to deep conversations. When she, at first, balked at what was demanded of her, she was shown the alternative and she quickly acquiesced to the group's demands. To maintain their air of authority, Ilya and Shar held themselves aloof from the general population of the gang and limited their sharing of themselves to the three original men in the group. That this created a form of Politburo, the women knew, but it also left them only having to exert control over the three men to control the entire group.

It was Shar that brought up an important point when they were deep in discussion about where to go next for food. "You know people, we are going about this all wrong. To get food, we need to go where the food is. Food is king now. That cash you have been taking off people we find has no meaning. There is no market for dollars anymore. A million of them won't buy you a pound of food of any kind. We can, and have traded some guns to some of the people we've met, but that is dangerous. Those fools could well use them against us as easily as not." When the shout came out about where to find food, Shar continued. "The Mormons! They have food. They horde food. Their leaders told 'em to stash it away so they been hiding it away for a long time."

"But that's our food too," came from the pack. "We deserve to live too, don't we? Ain't no reason those creeps should have it all and we don't have nuthin is they?"

52

Shar smiled while the group built themselves into a frenzy over the Mormons stealing their food then she called them to order. "They got gas too, if we know where to look," knowing this would further build the flames of hatred against a people none had known anything about beyond a few rumors just minutes before.

"I'll bet they keep that food in their churches," the one called Chico shouted out. "Prolly got tons of it stored up in the basements of their churches and sitting there laughing at us while they're living high and free on our stuff. Why, I'll bet they got all kinds of stuff they stole from us..."

That he had never owned anything bigger than a meth pipe in his entire life never entered Chico's mind and he certainly didn't allow that small fact to cloud his self-roused hatred for those who would steal what was rightfully his own!

When the leadership thought the fever had about built to a peak, they called the group to order, ordering Chico and the others to sit down and listen. While Shar and Ilya didn't know where all this bounty was actually stored, they did think that if they found it, they would have to fight to get it away from the thieves. After spurring the gang to action, they made their way to the Mormon church building that was nearest their location, near what used to be a major highway through town. No one knew quite what to expect when they arrived but what they found was not it.

Unfortunately for the gang, there was nothing different here than what they had been finding at every place they had been... ruins. Here as everywhere else they had been, the church building was devastated. Further, there was no sign of anyone having been searching in the devastation.   If there had been anything stored within, it would appear that it had to still be where it was left.   For more than two hours the searchers dug through the trash that remained until they found, at last, an access door they thought might lead to a hidden basement.   It was the work of but moments to break into the storage area and found exactly that... stored records.   There was no food to be found here and there was no indication anything had been removed.   What the gang did find was a potentially good shelter for them.   The basement was substantial and it appeared to be virtually intact.

While the group sat in their handiwork and discussed what they had not found, one of them came up with the idea that if they didn't store their food here, it must be in their homes.   "That's a great concept," Shar said with a snarl in her voice, but how the hell do we know where their homes were? They sure as hell aren't there now, dildo!"

"Well," Bart said, tentatively, "maybe there is something here that would tell where they live."

Ilya's head popped up and she leaped to a shelf she had seen in the back of the basement and she rummaged around in a box she had seen earlier in her search. What she came out with was a directory of members with their names, addresses and phone numbers.   Of course, the phone numbers meant nothing and the names were not important either, the fact that the book gave the addresses of every member was a great boon.

"Listen people, we are at Fifth Street and Union and this lists four houses in the five hundreds on Volland St.

That's only a block away," the girl said excitedly. "Come on, let's go."

In this area, the house numbers were written on the curbs before the individual homes. This was fortunate for there was certainly nothing about the homes that would identify them as to street address. Almost at once, Shar and Ilya sent guys in teams of two to investigate the four houses she had identified. In two, there was no food found, but one had a supply of bottled water stacked in a corner of the demolished shelter. One house, number 535 Volland St. appeared to have once held such a store, but nothing now remained. Whether the occupants had carried it away of whether others had come after, the CA 13 people could not determine. They just knew it was gone and their search was in vain.

The fourth home in the group, 538 Volland St. was not a bust, however. In an intact basement they found boxes of canned fruits and vegetables. On one shelf was loaded with cases of bottled water and adjacent was boxes filled with a drink mix. Wyler's was a good product, the girls in charge knew well and they were quick to stop the guys from pilfering bits of it. One young man, one who no one in the group liked and who had been making trouble for Jane, was off to the side by himself digging through the items shelved there. When he lifted a large bag of Oberto's Beef Jerky up the light to see what he had found, he quickly ducked down with it. Unfortunately, he was not quick enough with it and Rob had seen what he was secreting away.

"What'd you find there, Josh?" Rob asked. "You have something we need for the group, dude?"

"Nothing special," Josh lied. "It's just some flour and stuff." He slowly turned his back to the leader and pretended to be looking through other boxes, carefully avoiding his stash of goodies.

Shar's voice was mild as she spoke, having caught the gist of what Rob and meant and responding to Robs head nod toward the kid. "Josh, what do you got there?"

"I said I got nuthin," the boy replied again.

The shot rang out like a cannonade in the enclosed space and the little fellow never felt the bullet from Shar's .45 caliber automatic enter his brain and probably never ever heard the sound of the shot that killed him. But, dead he was... and for nothing more than a back of  dried meat that he would never again know. "Get this lying sack of puke out of here," the girl yelled. "I'll have no one in our group that does not put CA 13 first. Is there anyone that would like to disagree with that idea?"

As the shock wore off the rest of the gang, each was left with his own thoughts but the consensus was that he was a worthless pimple anyway and if she hadn't have done him, one of the rest of them would have had to do so later anyway. Not lost on anyone here, however, was the fact that their leader, though a chick, was one tough broad and no one had any desire to take her on in any kind of set to. This even extended to her non-exclusive partner, Rob.

When the CA 13 team had cleared out the goodies from the basement and moved them back to the church basement they had commandeered as their own, they learned the basic tenet of those who own something valuable… it has to be protected… especially from people like themselves. In the next week, the word had somehow passed to some other small groups who thought they were tough enough or who were desperate enough to want to take this cache. The ensuing gun battles were not long, but what they lacked in duration, they made up for in ferocity as the team defended what they had salvaged. They had lost one of their number in the fights but had taken out five of six of the attacking gang members creating a reputation as a group to be left strictly alone.

Late one afternoon following one such skirmish, the CA 13 was sitting around their fire trying to trying to get warm in a snowstorm. As the flakes swirled amid the ash still falling, it created a surreal kind of scene in the waning light. As one, the group was miserable. They had commandeered this place as their own and it was dry deep inside, but they could not have a fire there as the smoke would amass and run them out in short order. It was easily defended which spoke well for it, but it was a miserable place to try and be warm. Right now there was not a person here who would not have traded its security for some

Misery

warmth. All were remembering fondly the lack of misery they enjoyed before this thing happened that destroyed their world. They were feeling very sorry for themselves and despair was a palpable thing in their midst.

"This sucks," growled a very angry Jose. "If we gotta keep living like some kind of animal, I ain't so sure it's gonna be worth it."

"What you recommending, dude?" asked a surly Shar. "You got something better in mind, out with it. We ain't all so pleased with it neither, you know?"

"Yeah," Rob stated in that dangerously low voice he used when he was at his worst, "what you got on your mind? You unhappy with things here or how it's running?"

"Only thing I'm mad with is this damned ash falling on me alla time! We need 'nother place we can keep warm in. Jane's coughin' alla time and couple of the bros ain't doing so well neither. I was talkin' t'dude from over t'the river. He said they's a regular colony going on over there. They usin' the spud sheds on that big ranch and they gots food an a dry place to live an all. How come we can't have that?"

The discussion ensued on how to best go about doing something like that for them when the time was right. The outcome was, Rob was going to take a couple of boys and one of the girls and do a look-see on that place. Idle speculation was going to get them absolutely nowhere in this game. The girls leading this band knew that this game was life and death and if something didn't come down for them soon, death was going to take the upper hand. They were cognizant of the fact that the wet and chill was taking its toll. No one had been able to bathe or even clean up some in just ages. They had found a ton of makeup but unless they wanted to look like Jane, there was no use for it. It was time for a change and Ilya didn't much care how it came about. She and Shar had been spending more and more of their time together and away from the rest of the gang. They were beginning to believe they could live better alone than they were doing with this band of no-hope, wannabe desperados.

When the scout team returned with a report on what they'd seen, plans were made immediately to move in for a better look... The group had been able to scavenge a number of  semiautomatic weapons and hopes were high that their ability to get these into action would make the difference. The Recon team had observed that mid-morning was the best time as most of the population there was out of the compound and doing whatever it was they did. There would be the least people left there and once the takeover was complete, they could easily handle the stragglers as they returned to the nest.

With the plans set, the team moved out and walked as quickly as possible in the falling ash to the hills surrounding the compound. As they moved themselves into a position where they could easily attack those below, a note of alarm sounded in the leader's minds as they saw that their presence was observed and that the expected panic did not materialize. Shar looked at Ilya and together they stopped their advance. Let the fools rush in... the angels would wait their turn. If, somehow, the Cruz Azul 13 bunch looked like they could prevail, it would take nothing to follow them in and lend support. In the meantime, prudence will out, they would stay right here and watch what happened.

Already they could see the inhabitants scrambling, not in fear or panic, but in an organized manner to set up an obvious defense perimeter around their stronghold. The Leader girls watched this deployment in dismay and were suddenly very glad that they had made the decision to hold back. In fairness, it should be noted that, at this point, the girls did attempt to recall their troops, but they had moved out of hearing range and the little two-way radio had long since ceased to function. Whatever was to be was too far gone for this pair to affect the outcome. They were safe where they hid, so that is where they would remain...

Chapter VI
Attack

Colonel Kline quickly mustered his people and set them underway in the gray day to their assigned posts. The defense team had drilled often enough over the past week to know their places and their duties and there was not a person there, male or female, who was not prepared to perform their assigned function. They were well armed. Most carried the

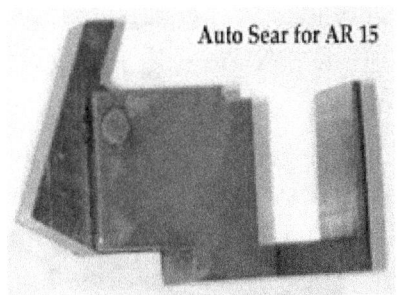

Auto Sear for AR 15

civilian AR 15 version of the military M-16... with one major alteration. All had been retrofitted with the drop in automatic sear that changed them from a semi-automatic rifle that required a separate pull of the trigger to fully automatic fire. All had been instructed in the safe and effective use of the weapon. There were none but knew the value of the weapons they carried.

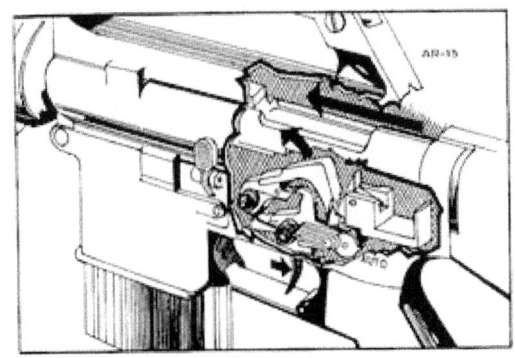

AR-15 WITH DROP-IN AUTO-SEAR

On the extreme corners, angling across the field of fire were two B.A.R. 30 caliber automatic rifles that had been found in the basement of an obvious collector in the Richland area. They were part of an extensive collection of World War Two weapons that was housed in four large fireproof and, obviously, asteroid proof gun safes that were found in a bunker-like basement. The place was virtually a bomb shelter but it had not seemed to have helped whoever lived there for no persons were found anywhere near it. Perhaps they had been caught away from their haven or had merely been asleep upstairs with no warning of the impending doom. These BARs were first introduced in 1918 in time for the First World War... the "War to End All Wars"... and were widely used in the next three wars after that. In WW II and Korea, they were used as part of a team described by one veteran as consisting of seven men... "One shooter, one loader and five men running for ammunition!" The venerable weapon fired the standard .30'06 round at a full fire rate of Six-Hundred Fifty rounds per minute. In other words, it put down a field of fire that made approach a very chancy thing. When placed such that two weapons fired across the killing fields at a forty-five degree angle, their effectiveness was increased many fold.

The defense squad was in place and ready when they saw four people walking out from the colony, seemingly to confront the approaching force some distance out. When Andy Kline raised his binoculars to his eyes to identify those doing this deed, he groaned aloud. "Who are those fools and what do they think they are doing?" growled the man on Andy's right side.

"It's that damned Johnston group," the Colonel responded. "I guess they think they're going to stop that gang from attacking." Andy fell silent as he watched the family split as Gerald left Marsha and his younger son behind while he and Drew advanced, one hand held high to show he was unarmed.

As they neared the advance group, Gerald spoke up. "People, I don't know why you are here, but we are sensible people here and this is not necessary."

Without preamble, two shots rang out from the gang on the hill and Gerald and Drew Johnston fell to the ground, the falling ash slowly beginning its task of covering what remained. Before the gang could consider their move towards the two remaining people further down the hill, the younger son literally carried his mother across a berm of ash and into the relative safety of a ditch-like depression. Fortunately it led them back in the direction of the colony and more safety than they could enjoy here in the falling sky. Quickly, Jase forced his mother down the ditch to the compound where people pulled them inside the building and offered them solace.

"They didn't even listen to him," a distraught Marsha Johnston screamed. "He might as well have been a mute for all the attention they paid him. That is so wrong, those people are not humans; they are animals."

"No, Marsha," a soft voice replied, "they are indeed humans. That, however, does not make them either humane or kind. They have their own set of rules they operate under. To them, it's simply the law of the jungle. The survival of the fittest is their only law. There is no justice outside of what is just for them and they will continue in this way as long as they don't run into someone bigger and stronger."

"But that is so against human nature," Marsha mumbled, her terror abating somewhat. "We do not live that way anymore. That was left behind with Genghis Khan and the Mongol Hordes. This is a land of civilized people. There is simply no reason to be shooting one another."

"Marsha," the voice continued reasonably, "there is no such thing as 'human nature' except to survive. We live, eat and survive within the mores of the society wherein we live. Our 'nature' is determined by that society. In a society of thieves, thievery is common and accepted. In a society of assassins, death is accepted. To us, it seems reasonable to assume that others want the same ends that we want. The fact is, they don't! That bunch up there in the hills does not want peaceful coexistence; they want our food and our shelter. To that end, they are willing to murder every person here. You just witnessed the truth of that on that slope."

"But, it's so wrong..." the woman whimpered.

"To us it is most wrong, for sure," the voice continued, "but to those people, it is a matter of survival. Our food and supplies mean they can survive awhile longer where without them, that survival becomes tenuous at best."

On the hillside, Rob had taken command of the gang in its assault and was directing his team to the edge of the last hills. There was some broken, ash covered heaps there to hide behind and contemplate their final assault on the compound. The young man had watched carefully until he had determined that their entire defense was concentrated directly in front of the sheds. There was probably a contingent at the far end of the sheds as well to protect against someone circling behind them. That's alright, he

64

thought, we can over power those in front and then attack the rear guard from the rear... a perfect plan, he thought. He had seen no more than four people man that position, so he felt confident that his team could simply rush them and over power them. For security, he'd send one of the gang around to the far end to fire into the rear guard, keeping them in place until he had made good on his assault.

The gang leader sent one of the newer kids on the errand to the rear. He suggested the lad take Jane with him so that it would look like a larger force. They would have no idea that the woman was useless in this type of action and it would get her out of his hair for the time being. When an objection was raised to sending Jane, Rob rounded on the objector and snarled, "You want to question me further, Boy?" as he held his rifle steady on the kid. Looking around, he stated, "if there is no further objections?"

Rob gave his minion time to have made the circuitous hike to the far end of the Quonsets and waited for the shots he'd told the kid to fire into the position to lock the rear guard into place. When those shots came, he ordered his team forward at a dead run to the barriers the colony had erected directly in front of the openings to the two sheds.

Col. Andy Kline, being an old hand at this by now, had aligned his forces it such a way that they created a Vee with the sharp point at the crude barricade covering three or five people with weapons. This small group had one purpose: be seen then, when the enemy force came, fade back away and out of sight to lure the attackers in close. Invariably, they focused on what they could see and ignored the possibility of what they could not see. The result was, the attacking force was in open ground in the center between to the arms of the vee when the word went out to "fire at will."

The result was immediate and complete. Instantly, sixteen fully automatic AR 15s and two BARs spoke and the crossfire was horrendous. The attacking line melted like butter on a hot day. Within seconds there was not an attacker standing and few even moved on the ashen tarmac that was the patio to the Quonsets.

The sudden outburst of firing from the front of the complex scared young Gabe so badly he never even fired another shot. He grabbed hold of Jane and just held her, his eyes pinched shut against what he knew he'd see if he opened them. He was absolutely petrified and immobile with fear. He was not cut out for this gang stuff. He'd never been around them before and it scared him to think about how mad they'd be because he didn't do his job well enough. He'd only fired his gun twice and then was too scared to move. It sounded like a war started. He didn't know who won that war, but it sure didn't sound good for his side. The rear guard, he could see, was still in place and they didn't appear panicked, so he assumed his side had not done well. When he observed additional armed people walk up to join the guard with a totally casual air, he made a quick decision. He turned to the mute Jane and told her what he planned to do and asked her if she wanted to go with him or return to what might be left of the gang. In response, she just lowered her eyes and hugged the arm she had been holding. This, Gabe assumed, meant that she wanted to stay with him, so, waving his arms and shouting that he was giving up, he stood. He then reached down and helped the shaken girl to her feet and together they made their way the last few yards across the patio to the position of those on guard.

When all motion ceased on the tarmac before the structures, Col Andy gave the word for his people to move to the people laying there to ascertain their status. Only two were still breathing and they each were bleeding profusely from multiple wounds. There was no hope of their survival and the colony had not the medical supplies to make a meaningful difference so the order was given to give them mercy and both were dispatched. The many bodies where then moved to a common grave and unceremoniously dumped into it and covered. A quick, cursory search was made of the bodies to determine if any identification could be found. Any such found was cataloged and placed into a file of similar such in case someone came looking at any time in the future.

While all was being cleaned up and the patio returned to normal, the rescue party had reached the bodies of Gerald Johnston and Drew. Gerald was gone, but Drew was breathing with a strong heartbeat so rescue efforts began to extract him from the ash and get him back to the makeshift infirmary in the Quonset. The young man was not as badly injured as was initially thought, but the ash was making him seem far worse than his wounds indicated. As quickly as he was returned to the infirmary, his clothing was cut away and efforts began to bathe the ash away. It was only after this was accomplished that the wounds could be accessed and addressed. Though not terribly severe, there were several and each had to be cleaned and sterilized as best as possible. Infection was still the deadliest enemy the colony had and most of their losses had been due to one type of infection or another.

"Andy," called Mike Barnes, the leader of the rear guard after the abortive battle was concluded, "I have a couple prisoners of war here."

"Bring them up here, Mike, let's see what you caught," the Colonel answered.

"Sir," Gabe began, "Jane and I were part of that group out front, but we didn't attack you. They sent us around to the back to fire a couple of shots to keep those people there. We're not gangsters like they are, but had to hang with them to survive. We didn't have no food or nuthin' and that was the only way we could live."

"I understand that, lad and I can surely understand your condition, but," Andy said with a stern eye on the pair, "what can you do for this group that would make it worth our time to take you in?"

"We know where there's a helluva pile of stored food," Gabe responded. "That bunch found a lot of food stores and they been hiding it out. Jane and me, we know where it's hidden and we could take you there."

Andy looked at Jane and when he would have spoken to her, Gabe explained that she didn't talk and wasn't sure she even could. Both looked back in instant surprise when the red haired girl said, "It's ok, Gabe, I know how to speak. My name is Arlene"

The tableau held while Gabe looked on in astonishment that the girl spoke at all let alone that she had a name of her own. While he was trying to get his mind around this startling fact, a shout rang out from the front of the complex.

Chapter VII
Changes

"Horses? Where did you find horses?" the voice cried out.

"You know that little valley over behind the ridge with the lawyer's house right on top? Yeah? Well, there is a huge barn down there full of hay and these beautiful animals. Mrs Bailey who lives there was able to survive the blast but was nearly out of food and water so was getting to be in bad shape so we brought her in."

The rescuers went on to explain that they had found the woman riding in the ruins near the south ridge and had called out to her. She turned to them immediately and tears were in her eyes as she realized that she was not left alone in the world. Subsequent conversation with Abby Baily revealed that she not only had the horse she rode, a rather incongruous mount who was actually a rather large, rather uncomfortable riding Belgian draft horse but this one's mate and two mules who were all broke to drive. In addition, she had a large, flat-bed hay wagon, and a freight wagon. Plus, she went on to explain, all the tack and harness needed to drive them. When people expressed the fact that they had no idea about how to harness a team, let alone how to drive one, she just looked at them with a sparkle in her eye and explained that there was a time they didn't know how to drive a car either, but that had changed, hadn't it?

With a bit of instruction from Abby, the two teams were hitched to the two wagons and, with an armed guard riding on each wagon, they returned to the compound with an adequate supply of fodder for the animals and, eventually with

Mule Team

all the stores from Abby's place plus that shown them by Gabe and Arlene from the old gang hideout. By nightfall two days after the attack that eliminated CA-13, the colony had increased in number by seven souls… three human and four equine. In addition, enough food was brought in to supply the group for a substantial time and in their movings, two more potato storage facilities were found intact. The newfound boon was placed under the auspices of Glenda Sykes and her Transportation Committee and Abby Bailey was assigned to be the person in charge of all things equine. Her word was law as far as

Team Drawn Hay Wagon

the uses to which her teams were put and the frequency they were used. She was assigned a small crew to maintain the rolling stock as well as the livestock themselves.

These were too far from the colony to be helpful at this time, but they were populated substantially by tons of spuds that were immediately utilized to augment the

71

colony's supplies. Another was found that was not the Quonset design and had caved in on itself. When the search squad attempted to approach this shed, however, they were met by gunfire from whoever had squatted there. Rather than create a new war, the searchers merely backed off and left them as they had found them. More often, recently, this had been happening. Many of the spud sheds were thusly occupied and defended. It was not calming to know there were armed gangs of people scattered across the area squatted on these facilities that had survived with various levels of viability. But, that was the case and it had to be noted. The searchers did remain near enough by to survey the groups they were finding. It was important that the number of people so encamped and their status, capabilities and level of aggression be catalogued and a watch be kept on them lest they decided they needed more.

It was in mid-summer when a new innovation made life a bit easier in the compound. There had been a small crew working on this innovation for some time and when, on July twentieth, the anniversary of the first Moon Landing, a switch was thrown and artificial light illuminated the infirmary area within the community shed. It wasn't much, to be sure, but DC powered lights borrowed from a wrecked camper blazed into being, providing much needed light to a critical area.

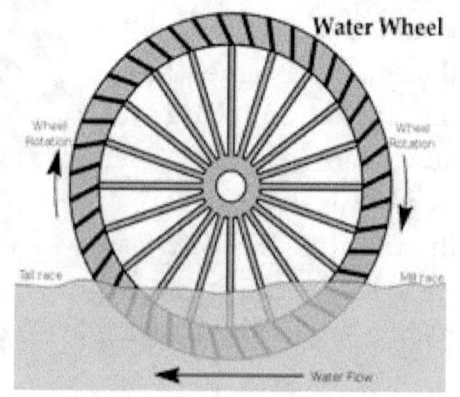

Water Wheel

Jared was on hand to witness this historic event although it was left to the discoverer and builder, Tommy Welch, to do the actual honors. When the young man was queried about his "invention" he stated rather matter-of-factly, "It is not a new invention, it is merely a new application to a very old system. All I have done is create a system to turn an alternator out of one of the thousands of wrecked cars around here and use that output to charge batteries we have scavenged. The output is a simple twelve volt dc system like is, or was, used in RV's to light and refrigerate them. The only trick was in finding a way to turn the alternator without using a gas engine to do so. As you all know, our attempts at resurrecting these engines to run in this constant dust has not been very successful. In fact, it would appear that, until this ash stops falling, we're not even going to be growing much food. But I digress…"

"What we did," Tommy continued, "was to utilize the old irrigation ditch that runs through the compound. We set a waterwheel we had fashioned into the ditch and measured the parameters we found. What we found was that with a four foot diameter wheel we needed six paddles for best performance. One of our team remembered from study that the ideal for such devices was to have paddles that numbered the diameter of the wheel plus two. Hence, our four foot wheel needed four plus two, or six paddles."

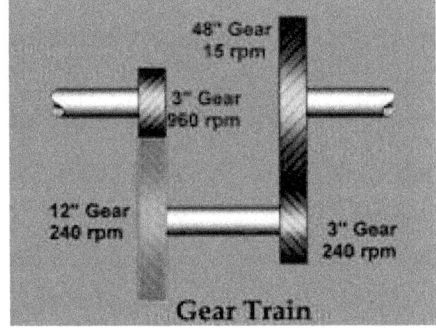

Gear Train

"The really tricky part came in getting the speed correct. From our observations we determined that we could turn our wheel at fifteen rpm in the water flow the ditch generated. We also knew that we needed to turn an automobile alternator at greater than seven hundred and fifty rpm to have it begin generating electricity. That meant we had to utilize a gear train to accomplish this step up in speed. Of course, when we step up in one area, we lose in another area, but that is more than is needed here now. Suffice to say, we found and utilized gear trains in such a way that we ended up turning our alternator a bit over nine hundred rpm. We achieved that by using a belt driven pulley system from our four foot wheel that drove a three inch diameter pulley on a shaft. Also on that shaft was a twelve inch diameter gear with ten teeth to the inch that was used to turn another gear of ten teeth per inch, but that was only three inches in diameter. This gear was on the shaft that drove the alternator."

At this point, Tommy's partner, Will Baker took over. "We then needed to decide how to use the electricity we made," he began. "Our gang talked about running this DC power through a chopper and converting it to AC… and we may well do that in the future, but for today, we decided that all we needed was the DC. There is plenty of equipment around that can use this power without modification. All the RV's have Direct Current lights and appliances in them. We have merely salvaged the lighting system from a wrecked motor home and utilized that. We have also salvaged a refrigerator and it is working nicely. We have stockpiled many deep cycle batteries of the type used in these motorhomes, so we should not run out anytime soon. We can place as many of these systems online as we need for our colony here and we can each have a few amps of power to make life a bit easier. Please remember, this will not work for winter as the ditch has always frozen over in the past. It did not this year but we don't know if that was a local anomaly or if it was caused by the ash cloud over us. Also, that same ash cloud may clog our ditch enough to stop the flow. These are things we will need to talk about as time goes along. It may prove to be too inefficient to maintain in the long run, but for now, we have some lights and we have some refrigeration."

It didn't take long before the colony learned a hard truth about using a horse drawn wagon in an environment where a wheel track is totally foreign. Add to that, the fact they were traveling through a medium that created and held a well-defined track that led right back to their home compound. It seemed that this led every outlaw gang directly back to their home. The result was more skirmishes of the type that the CA-13 gang attempted. While it was not anything that threatened the lives of those in a well defended compound, it did give the colony pause as to the wisdom of holding out here. There was very little that had grown this year in the attempts at gardening and the people knew that they could not survive forever on the food storage of the few people who had had the wisdom to plan ahead.

Colonel Andy had long since assigned shotgun guards to any squad operating outside the compound and a constant watch was kept on the circumference of the compound. No one in their right mind would dare attack this well armed and prepared force. The trouble was, as time passed and food was becoming more and more rare, there were more and more people who were not in their right mind. It seemed that almost daily, someone would try to attack one of the colony's work crews and, although there were no casualties among the colonists, it was wearing on their morale and made life more dangerous than it need to be. Something had to be done and, for the present, talk was all that was forthcoming. Suggestions had been made to go on a sweep to eliminate the aggressive gangs that, though few in number, were growing increasingly desperate and with that desperation, increasingly bold. This suggestion was shelved for the time being at least because no one really wanted to act the part of the assassin. The real problem boiled down to how would one know the aggressive, dangerous gangs from those just making their way in this aftermath?

Mark Moor stated that he felt they would all be dangerous as food became more rare and, while the majority felt he was probably right, no one was especially anxious to be the aggressor against them. Consequently, things went on as they had in the early summer. Learning from the intel passed on by

Ranch Complex in Canyon Bottom

Gabe and Arlene, those people in the various Mormon wards got together to identify all former member's homes so a systematic search could be instituted and their storage brought into the compound for the good of all surviving.

It wasn't until after the energy committee's little electric plants started generating surplus power that a light glimmered at the end of the tunnel. Finally, Bart Roberts had power enough to bring his powerful little ham radio online and begin searching the bands for other operators. On the fourth day, he located a station calling itself "Clyde Country". When he finally established a good link, he found they were a very small group of survivors huddling in hidden box valleys in the Palouse Country to the east of the Columbia Camp and much more remote. It was from this operator that a new and potentially valid suggestion was forthcoming... Why not do as the Children of Israel had done on leaving Egypt some three thousand five hundred years ago...

Chapter VIII
Scouts

Bart Roberts was so happy to have someone outside of the immediate area to speak with on his Ham Radio that he nearly forgot what to say, but as Bart himself often said, he was never without words for long and when he relaxed, it all flooded back into his mind. The summer had passed slowly in the old Tri Cities area and fall was now hard upon the colony. Their population had jumped to nearly three hundred people, a few dogs, fewer cats, nine horses and four mules. Abby had commanded a tight crew in training these new acquisitions to drive for there was little use at this time for an animal that could not help pull a wagon.

Bart talked amiably if cautiously with his new contact. This fellow lived well to the east of Bart's Tri Cities location in the foothills to the Blue Mountains. Bart learned that some of the large ranches located at the bottom of steep sided canyons had survived fairly well intact. Most  of them were de-peopled in the pressure waves that were associated with the horrendous blast but many structures

Ham Radio Setup

remained intact simply because they were located deep in the ground and the worst of the onslaught passed overhead. This was especially true of those depressions that ran in an east-west orientation. If the canyon had a north-south layout, the devastation was nearly as bad as it had been in the flatlands. This tended to support the contention that the actual explosion was to the north.

Mountain Spring

Bart's contact, Will Baylor was lamenting the fact that he seemed to be the last person on the face of earth in this far land. He stated that, other than his own wife, their children and his wife's sister and her family who also lived on their home place, there seemed to be no one else around. They had always been a bit isolated but this was now becoming a problem. Will asked Bart what the colony would say if they moved there to join them... for the company if nothing else.

The idea occurred to Bart in a flash but he did not betray his thoughts. Instead he said, simply: "Let me speak with the colony leaders and get a feeling for what they'd say, if that's ok?"

With Will's expressed agreement, talk returned to the desultory as Bart asked why Will was just now getting in contact with them. Will responded that he lived in the bottom of a canyon and, as such, he had little to no radio reception there. Of course the blast had destroyed his external antenna at the top of the ridge above his home, and this was the first opportunity he'd had to try out his system since he'd redone his antenna array. Bart very carefully interviewed his contact in the guise of simple curiosity while, in fact, he was extracting the information he knew that Jared and the Executive Committee would be asking him. No, they had no success with crops this summer. The winter wheat crop that should have ripened in June never materialized. Yes, they had large elevators full of stored wheat and other grains left from what was harvested last year and had not yet been shipped when the December blast occurred. No, ashfall was not a major problem for them though the skies were very, very dark all the time. It seems they were in a sort of banana belt for the ashfall. The surrounding mountains seem to split the ash clouds such that they were left in a kind of oasis. There was a ton of ash on the ground, but it had ceased falling just at the beginning of summer. No, summer did not seem as intense as it normally did in this area. No, he did not trust the waters in the creeks but he had developed two natural springs on his place and he had fresh water aplenty.

"I tell you," Bart said forcefully at the hastily called Executive Committee meeting, "this could well be our answer! I do not suggest we do anything blindly, but it is now into October and winter is coming on us, so we couldn't effect much of a change this year anyway. But, I suggest we send an investigating group… a scout group, if you will, now and check out what is there. I, for one, am heartily tired of living in this cesspool with its population of armed thugs trying to kill whoever just for what little they carry." When the committee seemed to assent to this, Bart went on, "I would volunteer for this myself. I have the portable radio I can carry with me and my ground station is nearly operational. I will train someone, or several someones in the operation of that set and we will seldom be out of communication."

It was a discussion that lasted nearly an hour, but in the end, Bart and three others, two of them armed defense forces, would be ferried across the Columbia River starting at Two Rivers Park on the Kennewick side and making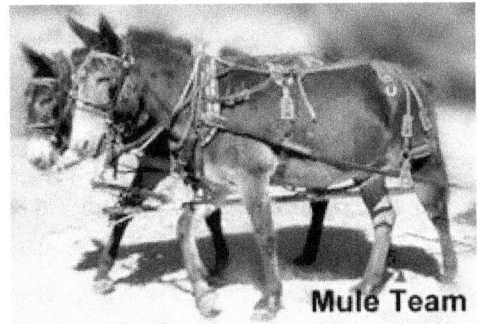

Mule Team

landfall as closely downstream of the Snake River as possible. It was decided they would follow the old highway across Eureka Flats and to the town of Dayton. Care would be given to investigating possible hidden pockets of similar undestroyed buildings along the way. Suggested areas were on the Touchet (pronounced two-she) River around the Lamar place and near Lyons Ferry Road area as these were both ranches set back into deep pockets in the hills. The scout team would proceed as quickly as possible to the Tucannon River canyon and, using the Hartsock Grade, descend into the canyon. The Baylor Ranch was very near the junction, just a bit upriver from where Hartsock Grade intersected the Tucannon Road. They were to do a quick survey and determine the feasibility of locating their numbers in that valley then return by the same route to the present compound and report. Knowing it was a trip of about eighty miles each way, five days travel time was allowed there and another five days to return.

It was felt that an additional four days on site should be sufficient to learn all they needed to know about the area. Spirits were high with a new sense of adventure and competition to be included was strong. Finally, the committee was called in to pick the scout team from a list of finalists compiled by Bart and some selected helpers. In the end, the team was expanded to six strong, including the two guards. The rationale was that with that long on the road, a good cook was essential as were two wranglers/laborers. With Bart in charge, Lila Simpson, a very capable pioneer type who happened to be able to do wonders with a simple list of ingredients and a Dutch Oven was chosen as the cook. Since physical strength may well be the only saving factor at any time on this trek, the other team members were all men. It was thought that they could use the old highway for travel, but that was not a certain thing and if they had to go overland, there would be streams and ditches to cross and brute force was often the only way out of the problems that arose. That there were some disappointed ladies was evident, but they made the decision and stuck to it. If this trek proved feasible, there may well be many more to follow. All would have their opportunities.

The route chosen would avoid major stream crossings

Swimming The River

after the huge Columbia River was behind them. Being fall in the inland empire meant that even the Columbia was at low flow and the crossing the easiest it would be at any time unless this winter proved colder than was expected. The colony closed ranks and together they outfitted the scout team with two waterproofed wagon boxes to float the wide river with all of their necessary gear. Enough scrap hardwood had been located to create bows for the wagons, across which salvaged canvas could be stretched to give the illusion of a return to the wagon trains that had brought many of the ancestors of those present to the west some one hundred and fifty or so years before. This design was revisited for one simple reason: It worked efficiently!

The colony had salvaged several aluminum rowboats from the wreckage of the city and these were used to ferry the people across while one driver rode each wagon as it was pulled by a swimming team. Two saddle horses made up the last of the cavy of six horses and two mules. Just as they were setting out, Jake Ryan's Blue Heeler decided he was not going to be left behind so jumped into the box of the wagon Jake drove thereby electing himself an honorary team member. The wagons were not loaded heavily as this was a quick excursion to check out conditions, nothing more. There was food enough, a barrel of water on each wagon, fodder for the livestock and their camp gear, such as it was... mostly bedding.

The entire colony turned out to see them off and when the teams entered the river a collective intake of breath could be heard as all assembled knew the dangers of crossing this wide flood. Slowly, the rowboats led the way with a strong contingent rowing each as they pulled for the opposite shore. Behind them the swimming teams were visible only from the neck up as they too lined out for south bank of the Snake River at its confluence with the mighty

Columbia. Although it seemed that they were being pulled downriver at a rate faster than they were crossing it, they were making headway and Bart called out to his team to pull hard and just keep their eyes locked on the far shore. On and on they pulled. The rowers were breathing hard, but not near exhaustion and the wagons were still being propelled by the teams and were not, in fact, pulling the teams down river. Their light loads meant they floated high in the water and so offered little for the minimal current to pull against. Time seemed to hang in the balance as the crew silently struggled onward. No words were spoken beyond those Bart spoke in encouraging the people to persevere! Even Lila was pulling strongly on an oar and the boats were first to grind ashore.

Quickly, the boat crews pulled their crafts up onto the gravel bank where help awaited from the contingent who had crossed earlier for just this purpose. It was known that the scout team would need time to hide their boats and gear up for the overland trek they had planned and, not wanting to delay them on their trip, a team had come across earlier to secure the landing zone against any possible dangers and to take over the task of securing the boats, freeing the scouts to head east at once.

As soon as his feet were dry, Bart radioed back to his base that they were all ashore and that the colony could resume breathing now. When that word was passed to the assembled crowd on the river bank, a collective laugh and sigh went through them as they realized that, in fact, they had suspended normal respiration while the crossing was in effect. Bart thanked the colony for all they had done and for the superior planning that had brought them to this point on the east shore of the Columbia within a quarter mile of the mouth of the Snake… just where they wanted to be to start their trek roughly parallel to the Snake River, following the route of State Highway 124 on its direct route east.

Traversing what had been the town of Burbank, the team saw no life of any kind. There was only the dull gray ash that coated everything. It was even difficult now to tell where homes had been prior to the blast. The whole area looked like a thick, pasty, gray snow had fallen and had accumulated to a depth of four to six feet in the lightest areas and more than twelve to sixteen feet where the wind had drifted it against some type of impediment. It was through this bleak land that the team… the only color in a colorless land… traveled. Part of their orders called for them to scout for items potentially useful to the colony as a whole. Not only food supplies were included in this, but so were tools, animals and even people.

In what had so recently been a land of green, rich, irrigated farmland, there was nothing but gray. Nothing grew there. There was nothing that was not gray as far as anyone could see in any direction. It was most disconcerting to the team to think that this was all there was. Slowly they moved along, allowing the stock teams to set the pace. Travel, while not easy, was not overly difficult at this time. The highway was buried in ash, but it was, nonetheless, still highly visible and served as a solid base beneath the ash they rode on. One hour had passed when Bart sang out and called his mounted horse guards in close to the wagons.

"Listen guys," he began, "there is a compound ahead of us just a ways with a couple of large spud sheds. Be especially alert around them. If there are any bad guys anywhere around, they are most apt to be holed up there. Just the same as we found those Quonsets to be so useful, so would someone else and while I don't figure to dispossess them of their homes, I do want to be careful in passing them."

So it was that the defense squad rode out first, to approach the sheds quietly and to read what was around. As it was, they need not have bothered. There was not a single person to be found anywhere around. Investigation showed the sheds to be nearly full. Inside those two sheds was enough food to keep the colony going for several years if they could be kept viable. Instantly, Bart was on his radio and in communication with his base, laying out what they had found and suggesting the colony lay claim before it was lost to some renegade.

About two miles further on, they came upon the ruins of the asparagus packing shed on the railroad line. The building was in ruins... in fact there was little remaining to tell anyone that anything of importance had ever existed there... except for one thing. The large freezer unit was still operating! When the

Hidden Ranch

team investigated, they discovered that there was a diesel

generator with its own fuel supply buried underground still operating and powering the freezing plant. The engine had a huge, multistage air cleaner on it that had obviously been able to filter the airborne ash sufficiently for the diesel to still be running. This was immediately called in as well. What the colony did with it was beyond the scout team's responsibility. They had done all they'd been asked to do when they called it back to headquarters. Lila did, however liberate several frozen packages of very nice asparagus to add to her pantry.

Just beyond this plant, the highway entered the area where cottonwood trees had been growing in great profusion. The plantations were owned and administered by Boise Cascade Company who also owned the paper mill at Wallula near the Walla Walla River. It was a disaster area now with not a single tree that was not broken. Ash covered the ground so it was impossible to tell if the young trees still remained, but there was no outward appearance of them, at any rate. It was an eerie kind of Hell the team rode through and even though the day was beginning to wane, it was decided to push on a bit further before making night camp. The team knew that Tagaris Farms "Snake River Vineyards" lay just beyond these cottonwood plantations and that sounded like a much better idea for a campground.

The mottled coming of daylight found the team up and moving. A quick breaking of their night's fast and the teams were hitched with the ease of experience and with Bart riding astride today, the scouts moved out smartly. Although the many thousands of acres of concord grapes no longer existed and the gently rolling landscape seemed safe enough from ambush, the two shotgun guards remained vigilant and did not become involved in the easy lethargy that seemed to envelope the rest of the scout team this day.

Midday found the little armada pulling out of the lower country in the vicinity of the old Broetje Orchards up onto the table lands of Eureka Flats. Lila let her mind flash back to before the blast when this was a thriving community. Ralph Broetje had created a very worthwhile entity here by providing permanent housing for his more than one thousand full time employees as well as his nearly three thousand seasonal workers. He had created schools, shopping and medical care right on the ranch, precluding the need for his people to make the sixty to seventy mile round trip into town. He had even established a home for troubled teens on his grounds. It appeared to be all gone now but that did not negate the significant effort it truly had been. The woman determined that, at the very least, she was going to erect a monument of sorts that would tell those who came later, if there be any, what had been done here.

The team rode aware through here as they knew there had been a sizable population at the orchards before the blast and there were four large potato sheds just at the edge of the flats. There wasn't a person here that didn't realize that if danger were to come, it would likely be near this source of food and shelter. When nothing materialized, one could sense a virtual easing of tension as they rode on past. A cursory inspection revealed that all of the sheds were full of spuds and only one had a door which was open. The scouts did not want to spend time here, but Bart did take time to call this in to the colony as the wagons rolled through. He recommended that Jared send out a team to secure this location against future need.

As the team continued east past the remains of the Agri-Northwest offices and yard Lila remembered that a deep coulee intercepted and crossed the path of the highway they were traveling just before reaching the Touchet North Road. To her, this memory brought a shiver of fear. She considered it very strange that no one was left in all this area... that the potato shed had been entered suggested there was a remnant population here but not having seen anything of them was ringing alarm bells in her brain.

As she called a short halt, she gathered their small group together and explained her feelings. No one was eager to deny the possibility as they were all veterans of more skirmishes than they cared to remember. It was an alert and wary crew that moved out from that hastily convened pow wow and not a single person was complacent. The drivers knew that their job was to drive. Lila, at the break, had taken over the reins of the lead wagon to free up another gun. Both shotgun guards preferred the freedom of being mounted on their saddle horses but the rest secreted themselves inside the wagon boxes. Just as they moved out, the canvas was rolled up just enough at both sides to allow vision from within the box. Thus prepared, the team rolled.

It was as if Lila had a form of foresight as a small force charged out of the cover of the dry coulee to attack the wagons. At first it appeared there were only a couple of attackers, but soon more were apparent and, at a sharp command, the wagons surged forward and through the small band of attackers. One attacker had jumped in front of the lead team to grab the reins and stop the charging beasts. He went down immediately before the flailing hooves of the huge Belgian draft horses and his screams had barely ceased when the hooves of the following mule team struck him solidly. He did not so much as wiggle.

In the brief instant of inaction afforded by this person's violent demise, the guards noticed that there were only two guns evident among the eight or nine attackers so each concentrated on one of those. A quick burst from their AR 15s ended the attack abruptly. As the three who had ridden in the boxes remained in hiding while the teamsters brought their charges to a halt just beyond the range of the motley band of wannabe brigands, the guards quickly took charge and herded the band to a safe spot off the berm that crossed the coulee lest there be more attackers still ensconced in the folds of the hideout.

It was the work of but a few moments to learn that these poor scums were all that remained of the population of the entire area. The community at Broetje was no more. The only survivors in the area were a few people here and there. The four large spud sheds had saved a very few people and here and there, a house that was especially protected had survived but this was very rare. Of those who had managed to survive the initial blast, several had succumbed to injury sustained in that blast, a few more due to contaminated food or water after the blast and several were lost to the gang warfare that had erupted here.

The attackers the scouts had captured looked very much like feral people. They were wild in their appearance and totally unkempt. They snarled almost like animals and their speech was almost incoherent. When Bart tried to isolate the leader of the group, he was at a loss until one female came forward who didn't look quite as bad as the rest. In fact she appeared quite clean for her situation. When he had questioned her a bit, he found that she had been alone until very recently.

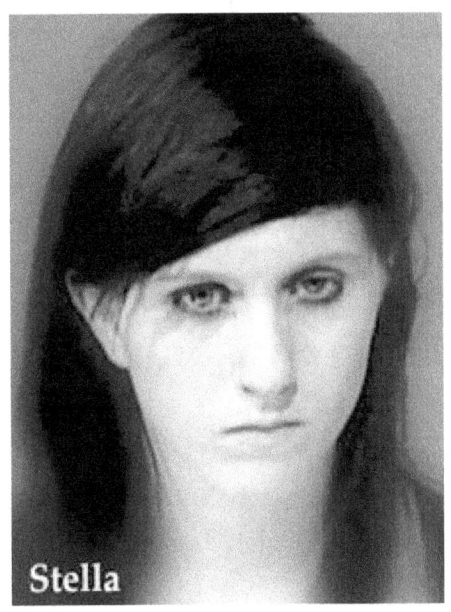

Stella

Her name was Stella and she had lived in a small house up a deep cut across from the Lamar Ranch. She had been the sole survivor of a family of eight souls and she had stayed in the ruins of her family home until her food had waned. Finally, with nothing to keep her on the place, she loaded a small pack with her remaining food and water and, taking her personal forty caliber Glock handgun, her brother's AK-47 replica along with enough ammunition for both to fight a small war, she set off on foot to try and make it to the Tri Cities in hope of finding someone still alive as well as food and drinkable water.

It was a gloomy walk under the dark and leaden sky. On and on she labored through the accumulated ash, moving steadily westerly. When she reached the four spud sheds west of Eureka Flats, she hesitated. She knew this was food and thought, correctly, that if there were any survivors in the area, they would home in on this food supply. She opened one of the sheds and moved in... inside, she found several cases of bottled water, bottled pop and even a few cases of beer in a storage room off to one side.

Life here was lonely, but not unendurable. She spent her time devising ways to improve her situation and in finding alternatives to a steady potato diet. She had copious quantities of wheat from the elevators here, but no way to grind it for flour so she devised a mortar and pestle system which she used to augment her simple diet. She found she could boil the wheat as well and eat it like a cooked cereal. Life was far from perfect, but it was life and there was so little of that left anywhere.

Bart admired the girl's pluck and asked her what she wanted to do now. He offered, after consultation with the rest of his team, the opportunity to travel with him and the team. She had the option of remaining where she was and they would pick her up on their return trip, or she could simply go her own way. That she had no commonality with her associates was obvious as they were more wild than human.

When Stella opted to travel with them, and even to show them through her country, the team was pleased and plans for immediate departure were made. The remaining weapons were confiscated from the feral beings and they were turned loose. When released they sped out of the area as rapidly as they could, not even looking back towards the now departing wagons.

Evening found the team just at the Lamar Ranch on the Touchet River. The river water was not to be trusted, but there were two sizable springs in the basalt bluff that formed the south bank of that river and the water from them would be good. The ranch house was gone but the old cabin that  dated back to the mid-1800s was there and intact. It was made of squared cottonwood logs and somehow had survived while the two main houses and the

Lamar Cabin on Touchet River

barn had not. There was an equipment shed across the river and next to a substantial bluff that appeared to be mostly intact, however. Stella stated that there was a Quonset down river a bit from the ranch yard so while dinner was being prepared, Bart took a saddle horse and, with Stella, went to investigate.

The shed was, indeed, there and intact. When the pair found a way in, they were quite amazed to find a full shed of old, horse drawn farm implements. The Lamar family had evidently kept these from the days they were used regularly and had preserved them inside this out-of-the-way storage shed. There was naught to be done presently, but Bart gave the girl a warm hug for her help in finding this and was surprised by the vehemence by which it was returned. As he held the girl, he looked down to her upturned face and was surprised when she reached up and kissed him. When he would have dissembled to her, she placed her finger on his lips and told him exactly how she felt about all he had done for her. Obviously she was more relieved by her rescue than the man had realized.

On the way back to camp, the girl clung tightly to the man from her position behind his saddle. It was far more than fear of falling off a horse, he thought, that made her cling so tightly. Oh well, he thought, I'm lonely too, so whatever is, is! There need be no more than that for sure!

Their evening camp was most pleasant. Here, beside the river, in the lee of high hills, the ashfall was at a minimum and they could actually sit out and enjoy the evening, however dark and gloomy the constant cover made it. It was not late when the fire had burned down and the early coming of night had chased the scouts to their beds. Smiles touched the lips of the team when Stella followed the quiet Bart to his bed and made as if to share it. Smiles shone, to be sure, but no one was begrudging or denying this to their stoic leader. There was not a person there that did not respect the man deeply and if the girl felt something for him, so be it. It was high time someone realized what a fine person he was. As for Bart, he merely pulled the girl close to him under the blanket and held her against him as he drifted off to sleep. All these months since his own wife had been lost in the impact had not caused him to forget how to appreciate the feeling of a warm, caring, feeling person next to him... that she was the age of his oldest son was not important at this time. He didn't feel this would be anything permanent... she was just feeling gratitude for his helping her and when they got back to the colony and she met others of her own peer group, she'd move on to them.

Night was short and with the morning light came duty and chores. It was just a matter of minutes to eat a quick breakfast of last night's reheated potato stew and get things cleaned and stored against today's trip that all hoped

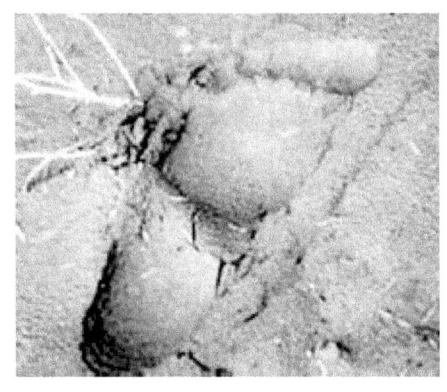

would find them on the Tucannon River. As the wagon was being loaded, Stella spoke out with a gasp... "Look at this!" she cried.

Quickly a crowd formed around her as she pointed out a perfectly formed imprint of very human footprint in the soft ash accumulated there. When the team saw the print, they immediately backed off so as not to disturb the scene while Eric Wiseman came forward. Being the tracker of the group, Eric looked at the print then began casting about for others. In the end, the located a very good trackway that came out of the water at the edge of the stream, walked up to and around the wagon, obviously stopping to peer inside at the goods contained therein and then on around to stand and watch the sleepers. Eric was able to point out where the individual who made the tracks had walked to within a few feet of the sentry squatted on his heels at the edge of camp. The trackway then continued on to the river's edge where they disappeared into the water.

Sasquatch Trackway

Speculation immediately broke out as to how this could happen with an alert sentry on duty. The remark was made that he might not have been all that alert if this being could approach that closely without being seen.

Interestingly, of all here, only Eric and, surprisingly, the young Stella knew what they were seeing. When someone suggested the tracks had been made by a bored guard, Eric suggested that person remove his shoes and walk the same path as was indicated by the trackway.

Doing so revealed some very interesting points. While the tracks left by the creature in the night were long, about sixteen inches long, and broad, approaching eleven inches in width at its widest, it did not show the arch of the person's foot. It was, in fact very flat-footed... or was it? There appeared to be a ridge across the middle of the foot running transversely... in addition, the front half of the foot was deeper than the back half. Looking at the print the person had just made, the obviously human print, the heaviest strike point was at the heel. Also, the left and right feet each made their own path as he walked. The large prints were in a single line... the left foot was directly in front of the right foot and the foot did not angle either in or out from the line of travel but was in a direct line. Most striking, however, was the stride. The human trackway, made by a man over six feet three inches tall showed a single

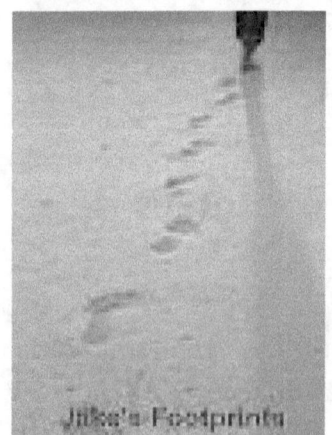

Jikee's Footprints

step of about thirty inches with a full stride of some five feet from left foot to left foot. The strange tracks in the night had a single step length of about four and a half feet and stride of over nine feet! This was an interesting find, to say the least.

With this fresh in the team's mind, Stella made one more telling point. "If this was made by our guard, how was it done? In this open, clear field of ash, as smooth as if it were snow, there are no other marks save the prints of whatever that is. How could someone of our size make tracks that are over four feet apart without leaving some indication? Also, if someone had fashioned some kind of fake foot of that size, where is it now? And..." and she stopped a moment to consider this point... "How did he make such a deep impression with that large of a snowshoe on his feet? Look at this impression of Jake's foot. It is nearly as deep as the creature's print. If he put on something as large as that footprint is, I doubt he'd even make much of an impression."

As the girl moved in closer to the image of the large print she stopped, her mouth opening in awe as she stated, "Will, be careful and come here. Look there at this print... there are ridges in it like the ridges that make fingerprints. Look over there at Jake's track and there are ridges in it as well but they don't look the same as these."

Dermal Ridges on Sasquatch Print

"No, Stella, they sure don't," he answered. "You are spot on. Those are called dermal ridges and they are, in fact what create fingerprints on your hands and fingers. Your feet have them too. You're totally right in that they are not the same on his track as they are on ours. This is most cool."

Bart then spoke out, asking for someone to make drawings as best they could and to record the data from the measurements and they would take it up with others when they got back. In the meantime, they had a long way to go and a short time to get there, as the song said and daylight was burning.

With that, the scout team bid a fond farewell to the tracks and moved out smartly. On the journey, Stella pointed out potential areas that might have survived. Passing the Lyon's Ferry Road, she told Bart that there were two different places just a few miles north that lay in deep canyons and so might have left some structures standing. Nooning found them near what used to be the town of Prescott though it would be difficult to recognize it as such now. As they stopped but long enough to recruit their stock and have a quick snack, they did not delay their trek for long. It was about this time that it was realized that tomorrow would be the earliest they could hope to see the Tucannon River, so resigned themselves to making a full hike today and leaving but a short stint on the morrow.

Hartsock Grade

With this in mind, they camped beyond what used to be Waitsburg and Dayton, following in the steps of the Lewis and Clark Expedition's Corps of Discovery as they camped on the site of their May second, 1806 campsite.

Again, it was the presence of live springs that argued for this spot. As all travelers of this genre knew, it was never wise to pass a fresh, flowing spring without making sure your water barrels were full in this land of little water. Camp was pleasant that evening and the night's guard was admonished to keep an eye open for anything like what appeared to have happened last night. No one expected it to recur, but one never knew in this land of desolation. As all were making their beds up for the night, it was Stella who silently took a bag of wheat and another of dried beans and left them with a small bag of dried apples. It was an expensive gift for the times, but it was important that she not stint to these Primal People she knew them to be.

Again, daylight found the team up and doing... the wagons were loaded and all the gear tucked away especially well for they knew that just ahead lay the steep Hartsock Grade that led them down into the Tucannon River Valley. In just over two miles, the elevation dropped by some fifteen hundred feet. The road wound around the hills like it had been welded there. No one knew what to expect, but the anticipation was enough to create a stir in the minds of all those in attendance. Before the team broke camp, Stella and Eric walked around, looking closely at the soft ash, hoping to locate tracks like they had seen at last night's campsite. When they came to the area the girl had left the food, she noted that it was no longer there. It appeared that the bags left out had been removed entirely, belying the chance of it being a common animal. Had a raccoon or a badger found the food, they would merely have torn into it and eaten it on the spot. At least there would have been evidence of their having been there. In this case there was simply no indication anything had ever been here.

Quietly, Stella told Eric what she had done and together they searched more diligently until just at the edge of a rocky scarp at the stream side, a partial track was showing in the ash. With a nod of knowing to one another, the two returned to their assigned spots and as the girl climbed onto the seat of the wagon she and Bart were to share today, she noticed something bright on the corner of the seat. Thinking Bart had found something he thought she might like, she looked more closely only to find a small piece of Oregon Opal tucked neatly in the corner of the seat. Stella smiled quietly to herself. She knew where it had come from but she would ask Bart later if he had left it, though she knew the answer before she asked the question.

When Stella did ask, Bart simply looked at the little stone and shook his head in a negative indication and told her she had made a friend for sure. She smiled quietly to herself as she realized the significance of that statement and she scooted closer to her man and held his arm as he drove confidently to the precipice of the grade.

At this point, all except the drivers dismounted the wagons and walked behind as the mounted horsemen hitched ropes to the rear of each wagon to provide a slowing force should a wagon want to gain too much speed on the descent. As luck would have it, there were no mishaps and it was an ecstatic team that rolled out onto the flats beside the Tucannon River and proceeded to the home of their hosts. As the teams turned into the short drive that led to the house built back up in the canyon, Will and Jeannie Baylor with their eighteen year old son, Justin and fifteen year old daughter, Jenna, hurried out to welcome the first new faces they'd seen in many more months than they'd cared to contemplate. Jeannie's sister Kayla followed closely behind with three young ones running and shouting in excitement. The scout team had arrived! It was a mighty happy group that celebrated there in the gloomy valley under the cover of ash filled skies.

Chapter IX
Tucannon Blue

A brightening morning found the Colony Scout Team up and moving. Lila had a hearty breakfast served even before it was light enough to see the shapes surrounding them in the morning gloaming. Together the team enjoyed their repast and the light camaraderie known only to those who have shared special times. As breakfast waned and the team gathered to outline the day's events, spirits were high and anticipation mounted. Even Stella, who was much more reserved than the rest... to the point that on the meeting of their hosts the evening prior had remained in the wagon, not wanting to venture forth just yet.

Sleeping Wagon

At home on the trail

When Bart assembled his team and Will had joined them, a plan was being discussed when Will noticed Stella for the first time. He stopped and reached out his hand and said, "Hi, I guess we didn't have a chance to meet last night" as he looked askance at her.

The girl smiled shyly and brought conversation to a total stop when she said, "I'm so happy to meet you, Will, my name is Stella Roberts."

For just a moment there was not a single sound to be heard from any assembled. It was as if they were in shock when suddenly, Bart grinned widely and said, "Stella is my wife, Will. We are newlyweds in the best way. As you can see, even our team did not know about it."

Time hung suspended for a few moments as the importance of this revelation sunk into the minds of those assembled. Promptly though, joy erupted from the assembly as what they knew to be was made real and given

Looking down into the Tucannon River Valley

voice. There was not one there who did not pray fervently that this couple would be the vanguard of a new society. True, they had not had words read over them, but did that really matter in this new time? Was it important that anyone approve or condone what these two people wanted of themselves? To be truthful, other than Jared back at the Colony, there were none who were officially recognized as having the authority to read those words, so this would have to do for now. Certainly there was no government, no law that would or could object to the action taken this morning by a young woman who simply pronounced herself married... and by the man who accepted and acknowledged that pronouncement.

It was decided this morning that the scouts would divide into two teams, one to go upriver in search of survivors and habitat and the other to go down. Will's children, Justin and Jenna as well as he and his sister in law Kayla would join the explorations. A thorough search had never been completed since the devastation and it was time for them to do so. Lila would remain behind with Jeannie Baylor and supervise Kayla's little ones and man the radio station. Will had his hand-held as did Bart, so communications could be maintained almost totally. It was decided that one of the armed guards would accompany each of the search teams and that never would there be less that two members to a team doing anything while away from the home ranch. There were enough weapons to insure that every member of both teams was armed. Of course the scout team was well trained in the handling and use of all the weapons in their arsenal and Will assured the others that he and his people were also so trained.

It was agreed that the teams would stay out at least one night on their quest and a second night was optional, dependent on what the teams found along the way. At any rate, the teams were to check in and coordinate their activities with

Team of Belgians

Jeannie and Lila at the base. For radio protocol and to preclude anyone else from isolating their activities and possibly planning an ambush, the downstream team was designated "Team Blue" and the upstream contingent was

"Team Red". No names were to be used, just Blue Leader and Red Leader. Each team member was assigned an identification number so that even their names were not aired.

Utilizing the wagons and teams Will had, each team had two wagons at their disposal and three saddle stock for outriders. That the Team Blue wagon had a saddle horse tied to the tailgate while its rider sat close beside her new mate in no way mitigated the feelings of others in their team. If Blue Twelve wanted to be near Blue Leader, so be it. The other Blues just smiled and felt good about what was happening there.

It was just past sunrise at the bottom of the steep sided canyon when the wagons rolled out on their missions. Team Blue included Justin Baylor simply because he could act as a guide in the area where he had lived his entire life. He knew the ranches and who lived there. He knew how many people were there before the blast. Stella had taken on the task of Team Scribe... as such, she would chronicle their trek, record what was found remaining at each ranch and inventory anything that might be of use to the colony if the former owners were not found. It was a slim chance, they knew, to find anyone still living, but nonetheless, they had to try. At the very least, they could lay to rest any lingering doubt as to who might have survived. That, actually, was primary in the young woman's mind as they began their trek downriver towards the mouth. Blue Twelve was also learning the use of her new husband's radio so as to relieve Blue Leader of that responsibility.

At the other end, young Jenna Baylor was, as Red Nine, serving in the same capacity for her father, Red Leader. Eric, Red Five, and Kayla, Red Three, were outriders while Jake, Red Eleven, drove the second wagon. For the Blue team, Bart, Blue Leader, and Sam Dowd, Blue Four, were the drivers while Eric's twin, Bud DeWitt, Blue Eight, and Justin Baylor, Blue Ten, were the outriders.

It was a very happy crew that wound their way downstream toward what Justin had said was a sizable ranch about a mile away. In the interim, several seasonal cabins were passed. Most were totally demolished by the huge hand of fate that had struck that long ago December morning. There was no sign of any person in any state around these cabins. Almost all were only used in the summer and then only on weekends. A couple would have been, undoubtedly, populated by people wanting to spend a pleasant, quiet Christmas in the mountains... a desire dashed so suddenly. Each cabin site was carefully inspected, however and where there was any sign of equipment, it was noted and cataloged for later exploration.

The Sparger place, the first large ranch was totally gone. The old ranchhouse that had been so recently abandoned in favor of a new triple-wide manufactured home was down, but the structure was not totally eliminated. The triple-wide was nowhere in evidence. It was as if it had never existed. There was simply no sign of it, nor was there sign of the Sparger family. Justin said this had been a large family of eight children, the oldest of which was a couple of years younger than him. He knew him well, because they had both played for the Dayton High School Bulldogs. The team did find, back up a narrow draw, an intact equipment shed and in it Pa Sparger had stored his two big tractors and an ancient buckboard wagon. In the tack room were harness and tack for more than this little buckboard so note was made of it and the team moved on.

Just beyond, on the left bank of the stream lay the ruins of another great ranch. All of the buildings on the flat were gone. The house, back against the hill, was a pile of rubble, no more. A quick search of the ranch yard revealed nothing. A more in depth search of the ranch house revealed the totally bleached bones of a rather large man. About six feet or so according to the measurements taken, he was found under a blown in door. That was the only evidence of any remains here. The Blue team had finished the inspection of the ranch yard when Justin and Bud came galloping into the yard on horses showing all the signs of being pushed hard.

Alfalfa In Barn

They had barely slid to a stop in the covering ash when Bud called out to the rest... "Come, follow us! You are not going to believe what we found up in the canyon." And he turned back around and waited impatiently for the other three to mount their wagons and follow along.

It was a most impressed team that pulled up to the large building they found hidden, nearly buried, in the steep sided little canyon. "I don't know what this building is for, but it is huge and I knew it had to be important so we came as quick as we could to get you," sputtered first one of the pair, then the other. "Look at how it's all buried down in that stuff. Before the blast, it had to have been almost completely covered with that vine stuff growing over it. Why, I'll bet you couldn't have even seen that from the air," they effused.

A thoughtful Bart didn't have to wonder much what he was seeing here. He'd seen it before. He knew why people hid buildings like this in such out of the way places. What worried him the most was what they were going to find when they opened the doors. He was not entirely sure that this building was going to be totally empty of people so he ordered his guards to the perimeter while he had Stella take Justin back around the curve in the road while he opened the door.

When silence greeted him and nothing more, the leader peeked around the gaping door to look in on a scene of unbelievable strangeness. As far as he could see into the building was a mass of green, growing plants... as well as dead and dying. That they were cannabis he knew before entering the building but to see it still growing was startling.

Pillaged Hay Shed

With a single motion, he sent his two gunners into the building, one on each side, SWAT team style, each ready to protect the other should the building be occupied. When nothing happened, the pair began a systematic search down the length of the massive space until they were quite certain they were alone here. It was not until then that they signaled for the rest of the team to join them. Before entering the building, Blue Leader radioed his base to report their find. A cursory exam and a quick estimate left him with the idea that there were more than ten acres under this roof... and millions in pot if there had been anyone left alive to buy it. Blue Leader knew that this state had just passed a law to legalize this... was that why this was here?

Although the find brought some titters from the younger folks, even Stella knew what this huge building meant to a struggling colony. She was amazed that the plants seemed to be growing yet although the building was not lighted inside. Further inspection showed bank upon bank of grow lights suspended overhead. Bart figured the

Remnant Elk Herd

building was on a timer system that would bring the lights up at night. He had found a sizable diesel generator in an equipment room off to one side. The fuel lines to the generator seemed to come from beneath, so when a cursory inspection failed to show a set of tanks, the leader assumed it was underground. Immediately, Bart tried to update his report to his home base but found he could not now get reception in this narrow defile so he called to his new wife that he was going to return to the flats to get a message back to base.

Absently, she waved at him and continued searching through the side rooms of the oversized greenhouse.

Before Bart had returned to the growhouse, Stella had located a backdoor to the building and, exiting it to see what lay behind this structure; she saw a second, similar door in the overgrowth just ahead of her. The girl immediately retreated to the front of the nearly quarter mile long building to find her husband. When she saw him returning to the great house, she ran to him to tell him of her find of what she suspected was a second such growhouse. Together they approached the second house warily. Although Bart felt the house was as empty as the first one had been, he, nevertheless, took no chances and made a second SWAT type entry.

Immediately on seeing the same thing here as they had found in the first house, Stella bounced to the back door to peek out once again… and again she found another house. With a squeal of delight, she let the rest of her team know of her success.

Before the Blue Team had left this ranch, four large growhouses had been located totaling a combined covered grow area of about forty acres, or about ten acres each. They had located an unbelievable forty acres of greenhouse to help them get crops started that would help increase their chances of survival significantly. It was a team of very happy people who moved on to the next ranch.

As the Blues moved down the river valley, they found less and less in the way of standing structures. Here, the valley was wider and not nearly as protected as it had been further upstream. It was so wide, in fact that the team

110

encountered an area that had been an irrigated alfalfa field. In all, there was about three hundred acres of alfalfa that had been growing here and they knew that there should be a sizable haystack somewhere.

What they found, actually, was several such stacks. Many, those near the open fields, especially, had been devastated by the blast effect. The hay there was gone... probably buried beneath the omnipresent ash, but when the team investigated the steep canyon behind the main house, they again found intact structures. In this case there were hay barns. They found two large, fully intact barns full to the brim with alfalfa from the previous summer. While the protein content in this feed was diminished, it was still fully viable for feed. A bit off from the two barns were two hay sheds set back into creases in the hills. These sheds were completely full as well, except there was one which had been entered and the hay was scattered... looking at the tracks around the shed in the soft ash showed that this was the feeding place for a number of deer and elk. Spirits were high when it was realized that at least some of these species remained alive. It had been feared that all may have perished in the blast.

Further exploration all the way to the mouth of the river, where it flowed into the Snake River showed no living being in all that area. Several more hidden haystacks were found, however, only a few showed the presence of animals depredating on them. On the return trip, the scout team, delayed an extra day because of all their discoveries, arrived in the vicinity of Marengo, a very old community, just in time to make camp on the second night out.

When a quick dinner had been prepared and served, Bart sat back with his new wife and looked at their surroundings in some detail. Having come from out of the area more than a few years ago and being one who was fascinated by geology in general and this area of massive basalt flows in particular, he marveled at what he saw here. The Tucannon River meandered back and forth across a slowly descending plain that was normally about a quarter mile in width and never more than a half mile. That river bottom dropped in elevation about four hundred feet in the approximately six miles from Will's ranch to this devastated community or a bit over a one percent grade. This created a river that was energetic and quick flowing, but never violent or dangerous. It had carved its way, anciently into the massive Columbia River Basalt Flows that were the underlying feature of the entirety of southeastern Washington, western Idaho and northeast Oregon. Over this base of multiple layers of basalt was a deep layer of loess soil. Loess is soil that is blown into place and is as fine as the finest ground sifted flour. Off this main valley were a number of smaller canyons that cut into the rock walls for distances varying from a few yards to a couple of miles or more in some cases. Often these side cuts had areas of smooth bottoms and the ranchers took advantage of these sheltered spots to place their outbuildings. They were out of sight and tucked in safely from the incessant winds that plagued the more exposed, flatter areas where the wheat was grown.

As the pair was watching closely for any sign of life on the cliffs, Justin came up to them and asked if he might sit for a moment. The young man was most polite and would never presume to interfere where not welcome. Slowly he began... "Bart, back up that road about a mile there was a large ranch. I think we might need to look at it if we have time."

Close-up of 4 separate flows

Loess Soil Blown in Over Columbia River Basalt

For the space of a few moments, Bart looked at the boy and then said "I think we need to take time, Justin. What is the layout there?"

It took the young man a few minutes to draw out what he knew of the place. He told them that the road continued on past the McDowell ranch and eventually led back to Dayton. The grade, he added, was steep from where they sat to the ranch but got even steeper beyond. He recommended that they split their forces here and leave one wagon on the flat and use two teams on the other one to negotiate the ten percent grade that led to the place in the hills. "I recommend," he continued, "that we leave two people here and three of us make the trip to the ranch."

Bart needed no time to consider the situation, he was quite sure the lad was right in his assessment and he felt the need to go heavily armed on this side trip. There was no telling what would be found here and he didn't want to risk his team at this late date. When he asked his bride to remain behind to watch the wagons, she objected, as he knew she would.

"Please listen closely," he stated. "We have very limited resources available to us. I need a combination of guns and strength to do this, and while I know that no one here is better with a rifle than you are, I need some brute strength on this outing. I also would trust you totally in regards to maintaining our equipment here. Add to that the fact that if I took you along with Justin, who I must take, that would leave both of our warriors in camp and I would have a tough time justifying that to a tribunal should something happen. Please understand this."

With a warm hug, the girl snuggled close to her chosen partner and marveled in his cold, solid logic. She knew that his decision was made with the entire expedition in mind, not just a desire to keep her safe. She immediately agreed and then, as soon as they were alone, she proceeded to demonstrate that understanding in the way of women to their men since time immemorial.

114

Daylight had not made its appearance in the valley bottom when Bart, Justin and Sam Dowd started up the grade with a wagon double hitched against need. The mile seemed to stretch forever in front of them as they crawled their way up the ash covered road towards who knew what fate. There were no structures standing between the Marengo Flats and the isolated ranch. Justin explained that he didn't think there had been any before the blast but he was not sure. "There are, however several outbuildings around the McDowell's house itself. I know they had hay sheds and silage towers and barns near the ranch house... but what else is there, I cannot remember. There were the two adults and, I believe, four children. I know they had a girl a year younger than me. We went to school together. There were two boys in grade school, I think then there was a baby. I don't know what happened to any of them."

Light had baptized the world by the time the three got near the ranch. Before entering the yard, Bart chose to climb one of the hills and, using his field glasses, reconnoiter the layout. He saw nothing moving, but all the buildings he could see were pretty much pristine. It was easy to see why as the little ranch yard covered a couple of acres with very steep sided hills surrounding it on all sides. There were buildings further up the small side canyon of which he could see no more than the roof in the morning light. By prearranged signals, he sent Sam and Justin forward to take up positions of mutual support should hidden elements prove hostile. Slowly the three men worked their way first to the main house, as this was considered the place most likely to harbor survivors. As they neared their objective, the kitchen door opened suddenly and a very dirty young woman stepped out into the yard. Her eyes were hollow and sunken and she seemed to not really be aware of the men around her. It seemed obvious that she was in shock and Bart wished now he'd brought Stella with him.

His "hello" to her from a range of ten feet or so seemed to shock her into attention and she turned her eyes to the man who had addressed her. Slowly, her eyes scanned the yard, finding the two young men standing alert and watching. With deliberation she turned back to Bart and seemed to visibly sink before him.

Sary

"Hello," she answered, I'm Sary Mc Dowell, who might you be?" Then, turning back to Justin she continued, "I know you, you're Justin. We went to school together."

Quickly, Justin moved to her side and got there just in time for her to sink into his arms as she folded completely. With Justin so contained, Sam and Bart moved in on the house with extra caution. They now knew that there was at least one survivor, so there could be any number more. When they opened the door and looked in, they were shocked to see over a foot of ash covering absolutely every surface within. In they went, like a conjoined team… from the kitchen, the usual entrance of all ranch houses and down the hall… room by room they searched and found nothing until just at the end, they opened what was probably the bedroom the girl had been

116

using and found two very filthy, very scrawny waifs peering at them with large, wondering eyes.

"Well, hello there, munchkins," Bart said with a smile. "I'm Bart and this is Sam, what are your names?" When no answer was forthcoming, Bart motioned Sam out of the room and set his own rifle outside the door and moved to the youngsters who appeared to be about eight or nine years old. He removed his handkerchief from his hip pocket and, using a bit of water from the canteen of fresh, pure water he carried, he proceeded to wash the waif's faces, all the time talking softly to them. "Are you hungry?" he asked quietly and when one of them nodded her head in the affirmative, he searched his day pack for an energy bar he knew was there. It wasn't much, but it was obviously more than they

Californian Rabbits

had been getting as witnessed by the way the little guy went to work on it.

When the other little one looked like he was about to cry, Bart broke the bar in half and gave half to him… and received a tiny smile in payment. By the time the bar was gone, Bart had learned that he was talking to Ian and Ann McDowell. He learned that they were twins and they were nine years old. They were worried about Sary because she was usually there with them and they were scared. Bart then took time to tell them who he was and why he was there. He explained that Sary was with Justin in the yard… did they know Justin? At another nod of affirmation, he asked them if they would like to join the others outside.

By the time they reached the yard, Sary was sitting on an inverted bucket holding onto Justin's arm as she drank greedily from his canteen and devoured some of his trail rations. The young man had learned that the entire family had survived  the blast but a quick trip down the hill to Marengo proved to them that they were probably unique in that respect. When they returned to the relative safety of their own ranch, the parents decided that Papa should set out overland towards Dayton to see if anyone else was alive in the world. Mama would stay with Sary, the twins and the baby. But, Mama had disappeared about a month ago, Sary said. She said she was going to go find some water for them at the spring and she had not come back. Sary explained that she had gone to the spring herself and there was no trace of Mama anywhere. Ash had fallen so much that there were no tracks left except some deer and elk tracks. When she couldn't find her, Sary returned to the other  three children to take care of them and...

118

"Three?" asked Justin. "We've only found the twins. Where is the baby? Justin was scared of what the girl might answer him when she stated that Patrick was upstairs in his own bed but he was not doing well as she had no milk and the formula that was left had run out about three days back. The girl was most afraid that the baby would not live.

Justin felt a surge of fear and wanted to run to find the baby, but he knew he couldn't leave Sary just then. When he looked askance at Bart, Sam said, "Let me go look," and he charged into the house and they could hear him running up the stairs. He returned shortly with a year old baby who was looking very wan and exhausted. He moved but little and whimpered not at all.

Bart sprang into immediate action. "This child can take some solid foods, but he is too weak now… he needs a broth… Justin, get a fire going while Sam goes to fetch the others. Don't bother with the second wagon, just use the saddle horses and get back here as quick as you can with some cook gear and food."

Sary told them she had cook stuff but not much food. When Justin told her that they had plenty, she broke down and cried into Justin's shoulder. Before Justin had finished speaking, Sam was gone, screaming down the grade back towards the camp at Marengo. Bart had left his radio with his young wife since he was quite sure he could not reach out with it from this deep hole. As Bud and Sam were assembling what was needed, Stella used that radio to call their base and let them know what had been found. She was most excited to hear that the Red Team was back in and they would be sending help immediately. Sam got on then and told them precisely what the situation was and before the conversation was finished, supplies were loaded into a wagon, a team was hitched and the Reds were coming.

In addition, Lila had insisted that Jenna take her place on the radio and she was coming as was Jeannie.

Will knew it was useless to try to get either of the mothers to stay behind when children were involved, so he assigned young Jake to team up with Jenna and keep the base station manned and ready. In  less than twenty minutes from Stella's call, the Red Team rolled out of the yard headed downriver to Marengo.

Guinea Fowl

In the two hours it took them to reach the ranch in the canyon, Justin and Stella with a little help from Sary had made a broth from dried meat and a little flour and had gotten Patrick to take a bit of it. The others had found a large tub and had built a fire to warm water. Stella had ushered Justin off to tend that fire and Sary stayed right with him. He said it was because she had known him before, but no one else was quite that sure.

Relieved of other duties, Bart and Sam resumed their search of the outbuildings and, about the time Will and the Red Team arrived in the ranch yard, they opened the end door on a low roofed barn made of steel. Inside they found

120

the most complete rabbitry either had ever seen. There were probably fifty cages with self-waterers and feeders. There were Rex, New Zealand Whites and Californian rabbits in the cages, a really good cross section. Inspection of the set up showed that the waterers were gravity fed from a spring that had been developed in one corner of the barn. The actual spring was in the rocks behind the barn but the elder McDowell had developed it so that no action was necessary to provide water to all of the cages. He had feeders designed for the alfalfa pellets commonly used as rabbit food. He also had a powered pelletizer for making his own feed from his own alfalfa. Obviously, that was inoperable just now, but Sary had been regularly feeding them alfalfa and making sure the water was flowing freely.

Bart and Will were most excited by this find because they knew that judicious breeding and care of a rabbit herd would provide protein and furs for a huge number of people from a small area. The two men were still babbling excitedly over this find when they opened the next barn to be greeted by three goats, two nannies and a billy and a half dozen sheep.

It was like they had found a gold mine in these barns and the pair could not wait to get to the last barn. Before they even reached the barn they could tell by the noises emanating from within that it held what they'd hoped. Bart could not have been happier in finding a goodly flock of Rhode Island Red chickens in one side of the barn, a small flock of turkeys in another section and in the back corner, about twenty five guinea fowl were squawking and strutting as only they can do.

As the men discussed the work that would be necessary to clean up the neglected barns, they thought about the best way to approach the problem of maintaining this property for the young woman and her family against the return of her family. They felt that, if nothing else, that they would move Kayla, Justin and one other, perhaps Jenna, to the McDowell Ranch and keep the kids there. For sure, Sary did not want to leave the home place with her parents both missing and out of any chance of contact.

By the time the men had returned to the ranch house, a good lunch was underway and the young ones had been bathed and dressed in clean clothes. Even Sary was scrubbed and dried and looking much more like the pretty young lady she was. As the two teams settled in to lunch, sentries were put out against any chance of attack. Discussion quickly turned to the exigencies at hand. Kayla quickly agreed to moving down to this ranch with her children and taking on the supervision and care of the three younger McDowell children. Justin volunteered to come with his aunt to take care of the barns. Jeannie wanted Jenna to remain at her home so Will turned to Bart and asked if he could spare a man for job. Without waiting, the DeWitt twins

ary McDowell

spoke up and said they'd be honored to stay and put this place in shape. They asked only that their saddle horses be left for them in case the colony decided not to move and they had to make their own way back to the area.

A nod from Bart and Will confirmed the agreement and those staying behind removed their gear from the wagons and began their chore of cleaning up while the remaining people began the retreat to the Baylor Ranch Headquarters.

The trek back was about three hours in duration and when the two team leaders were sitting comfortably with a drink and some snacks, Bart asked Will, "Tell me, Will, what happened to your team? What did you find upriver?"

"Well, Bart... we didn't have exactly the spectacular luck you had, but..."

Chapter X
Tucannon Red

..."We explored up the road only as far as Camp Wooten. That is inside the Umatilla National Forest boundary and there's no one that lives beyond there nor is there any permanent camp set up. I'm not sure if there was anyone in any of the campgrounds. There are wrecks of cars and trucks around them, but no people around any that we checked. Everything at the camp is pretty much toast."

"We found some farm critters surviving at a couple of the ranches, though how they did so is beyond me. The Benson place had three sows a boar and a couple litters of pigs. I brought them along and they are doing well in the barn. There are a quite a number of surviving poultry around. We rounded up all we could catch easily and left feed for the rest."

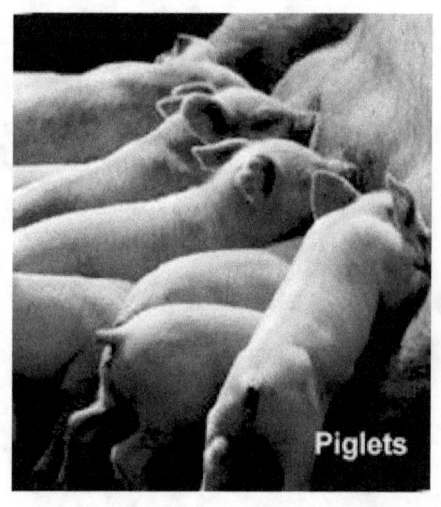

Piglets

"As I said, our searching was pretty mundane, but we spent time searching out some potential settlement areas. Our idea was to start locating places we could locate incoming families. After talking to you about what you found downstream plus what our Reds found upstream, we can house about two hundred people quite comfortably

124

right now… just move them in and set up housekeeping. I thought we'd probably do best by designating some barracks type of housing for single men and single women like the Israelis do in their Kibbutz system. We will need a standing protection force anyway and this might work best of all for us."

"As to that," Bart replied, "we have three major access points short of coming overland and down the cliffs, that's up from the mouth of the river, at Marengo and at Hartsock Grade. I'm sure there are a couple of other, lesser access roads we will need to guard as well, but if we cover those points, we are pretty secure in this valley."

"That's pretty much the size of it," Will responded with a slight grin. "We are pretty well out of sight down here in the bottom of this canyon. If we play our cards right, we can live and support a couple of thousand people in relative security from marauders."

"Getting back to what happened though… after we checked out every spot we could think of where people might be, we decided to divide into two teams and explore the side canyons for homestead sites…"

"Eric, who had exchanged places with Justin when the latter objected to staying away from the McDowell place… and Sary, would you be willing to take  Waterman Creek Kayla with you while I take Jake and Jenna with me and we do some scouting on our own?"

Eric let his eyes drift to the woman and when Kayla nodded in the affirmative, they both answered in the positive. It was Jenna who smiled and said, "Not without me! There is no way I'm not going to the Anderssen's farm on Tumalum Creek! We're a team and we can do it!"

Eric grinned at the young woman's exuberance and nodded back to Will that his women would be safe with him. "I'd like to go back down to Tumalum Creek as Jenna said and go up the Blind Grade Road a bit and see what is there. I think the creek goes back quite a ways and there is was a jeep road up that canyon bottom and I'd like to check that area closely. I know there's good water there... several springs come to surface there."

"Sounds good, Eric," Will replied. "I will take Jake and check out Four Mile, Waterman and Cummings Creeks. None of those are extensive as Tumalum and if we start early, we can be back home by dark. That said, when we split tomorrow morning, we'll just each make our own way back to the home place."

There were five people huddled around a waning fire before light began to make itself known in the land of the

Tumalum Creek

Tucannon that morning and not one of them but didn't know that they were in for a long day. They were traveling into areas that had not been seen by anyone living in many months now. It was possible that no one even existed in their part of the

126

world any longer and the team was worried. What did this mean for them in the long run? Kayla had lost her husband, the father of her tiny children in that terrible night and now she was setting out into who knew what?

Finally, daylight had crept into the bottom of the canyon and there was no further reason to delay their departure. Slowly the teams moved out... Red Leader and Red Eleven together and Red Five, Red Three with Red Nine forming the second group. It was decided that the wagons would not go off the roadways. Even covered in deep ash, they afforded a solid base and were safer to travel on. There would be no problem doubling up on the saddle horses for the time they would need to be away... it was just the sensible thing to do.

Eric and the two ladies made their way past the campground at the mouth of Tumalum Creek and moved up the road to Blind Grade. Rather than ascending the grade, they stayed in the bottom and quietly rode through the stillness of the morning. Amazingly, from time to time, they came on green trees. The three were a bit amazed to find these tiny oases of green in the gray world of ash that surrounded them. Most often, it was in quiet, protected, small valleys where the air did not stir much. In one such patch of green, the troupe took a short time out to recruit their stock and try to determine what was causing this anomaly.

In these copses, there was ample ash on the ground, though not as much as was evident on the plains outside of the canyon but the water seemed to run clearer... and even the sagebrush and grass seemed to be relatively clean of it here.

Just over a mile above the junction of the Blind Grade Road with that which traversed the creek bottom, the team came on a ranch tucked back in the canyon that ran north toward Linville Ridge. This ranch seemed so incongruous here. Why were there no people, Eric wondered nearly aloud. It seemed a sacrilege that such a perfect place and beautiful setting as this had to have been was no longer the home to people, for there seemed to be no one about. It was a subdued team that approached this tiny microcosm of what had been before that fateful December day not so long ago. There was a particular sadness that hung over this ranch like something one might reach out and touch. Kayla felt they were at home here and were waiting for guests to arrive... guests that were no more.

Just beyond the ranch was a rock scarp and, while the ladies checked out the ranch house and the immediate outbuildings, Eric rode quietly toward that scarp. He was approximately a hundred yards beyond the ranch yard, not wanting to separate himself further from his teammates when he saw it. There in the ash on the floor of the canyon was a track. It was humanoid, certainly, but just as certainly not human for it was huge by human standards. Then, looking

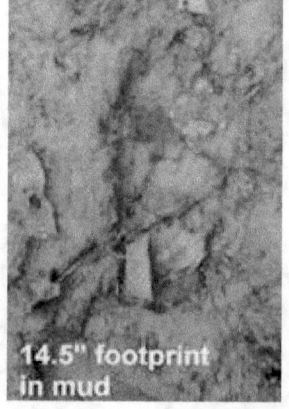

14.5" footprint in mud

128

further up the creek bottom he saw another…

Here in the soft ash in a remote valley on a remote ranch as dead as the people who once lived and loved here was a perfect five-toed human-like foot print that had to measure at least eighteen inches in length and was full ten inches wide at its widest point. In awe, Eric did not move, but just sat and watched the track like it might suddenly speak to him and tell him its secret. For the space of at least fifteen minutes, he did not move. Even his mount seemed to sense the solemnity of this moment and did not so much as lift a foot to move on. As Eric watched, it dawned on him that this was, indeed a sign to him.

Tracks were not new to the man. He was not a child to be confused or amazed by shiny baubles. He had lived nearly thirty years now and had seen many such tracks in his career spent in the forests of the northwest but this was something special. This was a notice to him as clearly as if it had been written in English and hung on the branch of a tree. It cried out to him. "Eric, we are here… talk to us."

Just as he had about built up the courage to speak out to whomever had made this image, he heard Kayla speak his name softly. Slowly he turned to see what she wanted, not entirely happy to have this moment shattered for him but not wanting to seem harsh to the attractive woman for, truly, he was seeing in her signs of strength and abilities that he had only heretofore dreamed of in a woman. She was smiling softly at him as she realized without being told, that she had interrupted something here. Looking beyond him to the place he looked, she knew immediately what it was. She lived in this place and knew these beings quite well.

Jenna also had seen such tracks before and was not surprised by this one. She stated that she was going to return to the barn they had recently opened and make sure the critters they found there were cared for properly. In doing so, she took the horse back with her for it was apparent that Eric would not be needing it further.

As the young woman retraced her steps to the barn, it struck Eric that he should probably keep all of his team together but, before he could speak, Kayla said quietly, "It's alright, we have been through that barn with a fine tooth comb and there is nothing dangerous lurking there. She then slowly stepped up next to the still unspeaking man and looked with him at the beautiful sight in the ash.

For the space of some ten minutes neither spoke aloud, but were existing only within themselves. Their thoughts were all that passed between them in the face of this marvelous find. Finally, it was Eric who spoke aloud. "Kayla, does this mean what I think it does? Why are there no tracks coming to this place and none leaving it… there is only this one clear large print and one clear smaller print where there should have been many if they traversed this ground… are they real or are they spirits?"

She answered, "Sometimes I think they are part of each. Why just this one track? What do you think?"

"Obviously," the man answered, "it is a sign. It speaks so clearly to me saying, 'I am here and this is my sign' that I cannot imagine anything else. But, dear Kayla, why is it here and why now?"

"Isn't that obvious?" she asked. "They want us to know they are about and they want the people that inhabit this place to understand their needs. Do you know that while there are probably two hundred hens in that barn in individual cages, there were only a few eggs to be

had? No person has been here in many months but that barn looks like it was tended regularly. There are poultry, rabbits and, on the far side, livestock in that place that are well tended. I had thought there had to be people coming here but now I know this is not the case... not our type of people, at any rate. If it were regular people, there would be tracks coming and going. There are none. Don't ask me how they do this, I don't know... but I do know they do it. We are on a ranch being tended by these large, hairy folks."

The air was alive with the tingle of suspense as Eric considered this information the woman had passed on to him. He would have loved to have argued with her over it, but he had no argument. What she said made imminent sense and he understood the inner meanings of it. He allowed his mind to work this possibility over for several moments before speaking and he then asked: "Were there, then, ever people here? Or, was this possibly their ranch?

"There were definitely people here," Kayla stated with a smile. "There was a large family that lived here. Olaf and Freida Anderssen had a pack of children, the oldest about twelve and the youngest just a baby. They were very friendly and helpful people. Olaf's parents were from Norway, I believe but he had been born here. So had Freida, I believe."

With a glance back at the barn that had swallowed Jenna, Eric suggested they follow just a bit further up the little canyon. He didn't want to leave the girl, but he knew, somehow, that she was safe and it was necessary he do this thing now.

As Kayla thought about this, she reached over and grasped Eric's hand and squeezed it. The look in her eyes was one of complete trust with something even more subtle lurking there. Silently nodding her head, she indicated that she agreed and together they stepped out slowly. There was nothing more in the ash to suggest anything had ever been here when they rounded a small outcrop of rock to see, not so far away, the mouth of a small cave in the basalt substrate there. It was not large, but perhaps eight feet high or a bit more at the entrance and not more than five feet wide.

Slowly the pair approached the mouth of the structure with great care and stealth, so they thought, until they could see into the depths just a bit. What they saw caused them to want to see more, so, as one, they made their way to the entrance and peered into the dark interior. First one, then the other stepped into the cave and marveled at what they saw. Immediately on entering the cavern, they saw that the entrance had been deceiving for inside, it opened into a large, open space at least fourteen feet high and the immediate room was probably four hundred square feet. That it had more to it was obvious for there were dark holes on either side that seemed to lead even further into the mountain but the lack of light prohibited any further exploration along those lines. As their eyes adjusted to the darkened condition of the interior, they saw many features that held their interest. Obviously the Anderssens knew of this cave and it was probably a major play area for the young ones as evidenced by the numerous human artifacts herein. There was a table with a few small chairs about it and a collection of shelves and benches around the space. It was evident this had been a very pleasant and convenient playhouse for the children. What was not so evident, however, was the reason for the myriad of large tracks visible in the dusty floor. There were tracks of all sizes from a half foot long to the twin of the huge one left for them down the valley.

Neither person spoke... the scene was just too overwhelming to want to disturb. Slowly, as if on some unheard cue, Eric and Kayla backed out of the cave and stood looking into the dark interior for a moment when the woman said softly, "Thank you for sharing that."

Almost at once, both of the people heard very distinctly: *"Thank you, please return when you are settled."*

With a small yelp, Kayla turned to Eric and asked: "Did you say something? Was that you I heard say thank you?"

"No, Kayla," he responded. "It was not me but I heard it very clearly. It was not spoken aloud, I don't believe, but it seemed to come directly into my mind like a message I might have received from the Holy Spirit. I don't know, but I suspect that our friends can speak to us without having to make sounds."

But that's nuts, isn't it?" Kayla asked. As she stepped to him and buried her head on his chest, his arms automatically encircling her and drawing her closer, she continued: "I mean, they're animals, aren't they? They're some kind of remnant ape aren't they? I've never heard apes talk to me though and whatever that was, it spoke to us. I know that as sure as I am sitting here. She decided to test

Rabbit Barn

that premise and she spoke again. "What would you have us do for you since we are here?"

In the quiet of the midday, it came: *"Clean out this home and live there. We would that you would be nearest us as you understand us. We have been living from the creatures grown there. If it is possible we would wish to continue this. We can survive with the help of the food available there if it is not stopped. Please help us, we are desperate."*

134

For a long minute Kayla and Eric looked one to the other before Kayla spoke out, first to them: "Of course. We shall see that you will have plenty to eat and you will be welcome here always." Then to Eric, she continued: "Will you live here with me and the babies?"

Eric did not delay, he had been attracted to this pretty woman since he'd first met her and he now felt compelled to continue. "Of course I will. I'm more than happy you asked. We will need to see the others settled before we can settle, but this is our home from this time on.

The man then turned back to the cave and spoke: "Do you need anything else from us now? Can you manage until we get the rest of our people settled and can return to take up this ranch?"

"We can," the voice spoke into their mind. *"We can make the creatures in the structures prosper and they provide us with all we need for now. We had the chance to learn from those who resided here before how to care for the small furred ones and the feathered ones so we will continue with it until you return. We will not let others stay here."*

It was quiet as the couple retraced their steps to the Anderssen farm and helped Jenna in her assessment of the rabbit and poultry barn. It was obvious that this was a very efficiently run operation with a huge supply of feed available and a never ending water supply from a live spring. It was, in fact, ideal for the large people living in the cave to take over and operate to their own benefit. When they had a moment they discussed the plight those primal people had faced with the demise of so much of their natural food supply. With knowing fully, it was surmised that wild

135

game and probably fish were important components of their diet and those were not now available.

Eric and Kayla sat together closely and explained to Jenna what they had heard and what they had learned. The young girl listened quietly as the couple stammered reluctantly through a description of the conversation they had had with the disconnected voice. She then said, "It's very much the 'still small voice' they teach about in Sunday School, isn't it? I have heard them often at home. That is why I wanted so much to come this way. I know they live here and was not surprised at all by what we found."

Kayla looked at Eric cautiously and then turned back to Jenna. "Are you saying you hear them? That they talk to you… not just today, but before?"

"Oh yes," the girl effused. "I have talked to one who calls himself a 'Teacher', an Ancient One, often. He has asked me to do things for them that they cannot do for themselves. I know the Anderssen kids knew they were here because they talked of them often. I suppose we all just kind of took them for granted because we grew up with them around us. I was most surprised to find out in high school that some people said we were just making them up. I tried to explain differently, but they just laughed at me. Some even said I was hallucinating… that I must be on drugs or something, so I just quit talking about them. I knew they were real but these people didn't and they wouldn't even listen which I thought was so bogus!"

When Eric reached over to hold Kayla's hand, the girl smiled widely and said, "Does this mean what I think it does? Are you two a couple now? Are you going to be like Uncle Bart and Stella?"

Shyly, Kayla grinned at the irrepressible girl and said: "Well, girl, it's early yet, but Eric is a pretty delectable hunk, isn't he?"

The girls laughed then at the man's discomposure and when he blushed wildly, Kayla and Jenna could not help but tease him even more. In fact, the young woman was most thrilled with the fact that her aunt had reacted this way to Eric. She liked Eric and his twin but was afraid she was too young to be taken seriously by them, so she had made no overt suggestions to them. Secretly, she had hoped that maybe one or the other would find her attractive enough to want to spend time with her. Unfortunately, she didn't really know how to go about it with a man. If it had been a boy about her age, she would not have had a problem, but the boys here age were such jerks that she didn't really want to spend any time around them. No... the young lady was not jealous of her aunt, who she loved dearly, and Eric and their new found attachment. She was, however, a bit envious that she could not take such an action on her own.

Together the three walked further up the ash covered road that roughly paralleled the mostly dry creek bed and located several more copses of green, growing trees... it was not coincidence, they felt, that these green spots marked the locations of flowing springs. How this accounted for the green foliage, however, none could imagine. It was obvious to all three of the people that they were not alone in this valley. They could easily imagine the feelings they were getting were caused by these primal people keeping a close eye on them as they explored the area in more depth.

From the ranch, it was about three miles to the forks of the creek and by this time the three saw no reason to go further. They had located several springs in areas that would make decent homesteads but they knew they would have to be so very careful in the selection of people to inhabit this canyon. In thinking about the primal people here, they realized they may well be dealing with a last vestige of a dying population.

If the devastation that had wreaked havoc on their world was so terrible to them, how much worse would it have been on these primal folks? They didn't plant, so had no ongoing food supplies. It was considered highly unlikely by the three that they stored much food, so with the destruction of their regular food sources, they were in a very hard way. While it was likely that there were other pockets of population who had found such as this group, those who had not had this opportunity would not likely survive the famine that was sure to have ensued. No, they thought, this was neither the last nor the only group left, but it was definitely one of the few lucky groups. They decided quickly that the preservation of this clan was of paramount importance and that this valley was an integral part of that preservation. It was at this instant that the first and probably the only Primal People Reserve was established. There was nothing in this valley that could not be emulated in other valleys in the area. It would cost no one anything to have this few square miles set aside for this truly indigenous people.

As the three people turned around and began their trek back to the ranch, Jenna heard a branch snap and her eyes were drawn to the small, green copse just at the junction of the two forks of Tumalum Creek. "Look!" she hissed under her breath. "Look in those trees. There is one of them hiding and peeking back at us."

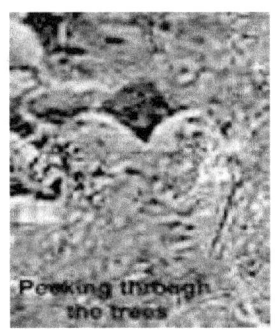

Peeking through the trees

It took the couple a bit of searching before first Kayla and then Eric located the dark fellow looking at them. For more than a few minutes, the three people watched in awe at the obviously young sasquatch as it returned the gaze. At last, the voice returned. *"This is my son Inisha. He is tending his sister Aranya in the manner of our people."*

It was Jenna who spoke up to ask the question, "What do you mean, 'in the manner of your people?' Is that so different from our way?"

"No, young woman, it is not," the voice responded. *"But in our culture, the older youth of Inisha's age are the child tenders. They begin at the age the babies can leave their mothers and it is this task that prepares the young one to have a family of his own one day. He must learn the compassion and skills necessary to sustain the very young. He must learn to cooperate with others of*

Jenna

his age and station to keep the young ones safe and well fed, dry and clean and happy and comfortable. This will, in time, prepare him to sire his own children."

It took the three people several minutes to locate Aranya as Inisha had her well hidden in the foliage. Eventually, however all three did find her and, making no overt move toward the young primal people, they watched for a few more minutes before Inisha stood and took his sister by the hand and together they walked back into the thicker brush. It seemed impossible to the humans for these large people to be able to move through the stiff brush without making noise or impaling themselves on the sharp stobs left from the breaking of branches by the blast wave. Indeed, many times the humans had tried to pass through these thick areas, it had resulted in some injury to them. The two women and the man merely shook their heads in amazement and watched as, just before moving out of sight for the last time, Inisha turned back to them and waved. All three waved back and said together, "we will see you again soon."

It was an exuberant group who finished their survey of the Tumalum basin and headed back downstream to meet the Tucannon a few miles away.   Already, they were planning on who they could trust with their information and who to recruit into their little sub-clan of survivors. Eric told Kayla that he had some prospects among the colony they were planning to bring to the valley on their return. At any rate, no matter what the colony planned, he would be returning as quickly as he could.   He was quite sure his brother, Bud, would want to return quickly as well.

When Jenna showed an unusual interest in this factoid, Kayla pegged on the reason quickly. As it seemed Eric had no clue of the girl's interest, Kayla grinned within herself and waited until Jenna had moved ahead enough that she was out of earshot. It was then she told Eric what she suspected and when he still dumbstruck, she laughed aloud.

"Eric, Dear," she began, "why do you think she was so eager to travel with us on this little trek? Do you think it was MY company she was after when she had that every day, all day for the past many months? No, my Darling... it is you she wanted to be near. She has never been interested in people near her own age... especially not those of the male persuasion. She has always been too mature for them. I think that came from being raised on the ranch here and being so independent in everything she did. Little boy and little girl games did not hold any appeal for her after the age of ten or so because, by then, she was hunting and fishing with her father and brother and running a ranch with her mother. She had her own livestock that she was responsible for and she did well with it. There has not been a year since she was ten that she has not harvested her own elk and her own mule deer, having a huge disdain for the tiny whitetail deer that live in the river bottoms here. She could and did prepare her own critters for the freezer and she could and did prepare and, since she was about fourteen, tan her own hides and make her own leather. Since she knows you are not available to her, can you guess who is her second choice?"

"But she is just a child, isn't she?" Eric asked in a quizzical way. "I mean, she's what, maybe fourteen or fifteen?"

"She is nearly sixteen... an age, I might remind you, that was very common for brides a hundred and fifty years ago when times were not so dissimilar to where we find ourselves right now."

For the space of maybe ten minutes, the man did not speak... he only thought about what the pretty blonde lady next to him had said. He had to admit to himself that, girl she might be in age, but she was certainly not a girl in body or mind. One thing he knew... Bud was in trouble!

The sun, had it been visible, was well past the zenith by the time three team members had returned to their left behind wagons at the site of the old "Last Resort Store and Campground" at the mouth of Tumalum Creek. Knowing the day was slipping away more rapidly than they had planned for, the scouts did not delay, but quickly hitched the team and hurried down the last mile and a half to the main ranch yard.

... The mood was somber when Will finished his narrative while a man might have counted to twenty slowly. Then, with a low, soft whistle, Bart began: "You are sure of what Eric and Kayla relayed to you about being talked to like that? I mean, do you think it possible for that to have happened as they explained it?"

Will did not answer the fellow for a few moments but thought deeply about the words he was about to utter for he knew that what he said now could have profound and far

142

reaching effects. Slowly, deliberately and softly he began, speaking as earnestly as he could while keeping his voice under complete control. "Bart, let me start by saying this about that. I have not known Eric all that long, but I have come to trust him and to, especially, trust his judgment or I would not have sent him off with two of my women. That said, you would know more of his truthfulness than would I… but…" and he paused here more than a few moments… "I do know the women in my family. Jenna is my daughter and Kayla is my wife's baby sister and she has lived with us since the girl's parents died when Kayla was about eight and Jeannie, my wife, about twenty or so years old. That was before either of my two was born. I would trust my life to either of those two women and often have. Neither one of them would ever knowingly concoct such a tale for any reason other than to tease someone for a minute or two. This is not such a case. Those three people are very serious in what they reported. If they say it is so, I believe it is so. It's that simple."

Bart considered that deeply before replying. "Will, I don't pretend to understand it at all but I have no trouble believing those creatures exist. We had tracks around us on our way out here and I know my wife is most interested in the creatures and she and Eric recorded all the

Anderssen Ranch

data about the tracks on our way here. I do not disbelieve you nor do I disbelieve them. If this is the case, we will need to make allowances for them."

"Bart," Will began, "I don't think that is necessary. They've been doing alright on their own for as long as we have been on this planet in our form, so I reckon they can probably continue to do so. But, let's call those three in and see what they think about this, ok? Oh, wait," he exclaimed, "Kayla and Eric are at the McDowell place... would Jenna be willing to fill us in further about this? Maybe Stella would like to be part of it as well."

Two hours later, everyone on the Baylor place knew of the incident in detail and what the trio had decided to do about settlement in the valley. Jenna explained that while she agreed with her dad in principle about their need for safety, right now they felt it was a critical time for them as all of their normal food supply had been pretty much eliminated. When Jeannie and Lila asked what they were living on then, Jenna went on with reluctance to explain how they had been carefully tending the Anderssen's poultry, rabbits and other livestock and subsisting off those commodities. Jenna was very concise in her explanation and paused at the conclusion to tell her mother and father of her decision to move with Eric and Kayla to the Anderssen place and implement their plans for the people that lived in the caves there.

When her mother started to protest, Will spoke up and defended the girl's right to do this. He explained that there was no more school to attend daily and since all had been reduced to subsistence living, she probably had all the general education she needed. Further, he considered her a mature person now, capable of charting her own course and lastly, this was mighty important work she was contemplating. Thus the discussion was settled and Jeannie understood and agreed with her daughter's choice. After all, she mused, it wasn't like she was going to be living on the dark side of the moon. They would only be a few miles upriver and so, close to home.

Will turned back to Bart and, looking around them, asked, "How is the colony fixed for population? I mean, I know there are about two hundred people in total in the colony, but what is the man to woman ratio? Are you about even or does one side or the other predominate?"

Bart thought for a few moments and replied, "Actually, Will, I think men are way in minority. If I had to put a number on it right now, I'd have to say there are probably a hundred and twenty or so women and about eighty men. So, I would guess it's about a three to two ratio. I don't think that women survived the blast better than men did, but I think more men have been lost in accidents since the blast and, of course, too many younger men think they can make their way with the gangs of thugs. Many of those gangs are woman free and the rest are very predominately male. We pick up a lot more women seeking shelter than we do men. If it persists, it may create problems in the society. But for now, it seems to be working out for us."

"I understand that," Will responded, "but how will it work out when they get here and they have to return to a working farm environment? Will the married women tolerate so many unattached women in their homes? Here, it won't be a commune type of atmosphere as you have in the colony there. Here, it will be a commune as far as work and life are concerned, but domestic relationships are going to very individual."

"Wow," Bart expounded, "I had not considered that but you are absolutely right. That is something the council needs to consider and decide on."

As the evening wore on, talk returned to the discussion of the trip back. Will explained that he had gotten a radio call from a new contact in Walla Walla. They seemed to have, he said, the same problems that were being

Lila... Will... Jeannie

experienced in most urban areas... a small colony of good people, generally getting by on stored reserves and purloined potatoes and being plagued by roving gangs of marauders... although these seemed to be disappearing slowly.

It was decided that the return trip should swing south to the town to assess the situation first hand. It was further decided that Lila would drive one of the wagons with Stella and Luke as the outriders. This would leave the DeWitt brothers free to stay and keep the McDowell place in order and open the Anderssen place to get the reserve in order. Soon it was time to assemble the return team. Bud Dewitt and Justin stayed at the McDowell place, kind of disappointing Jenna but Sary and Justin were now an official couple and did not want to be apart.

On the morning of departure, Will came out of the house with Lila on one side and Jeannie on the other. Neither wanted Lila to go, but both knew she was needed to make the trip back to the colony. Jake saw first what was happening here and assured them that even if the rest of the colony wanted to wait until spring to make the trip, he was sure an advance party would be needed to make things ready here, so he would return with that party and make sure Lila was with him. There were tears in abundance when the caravan rolled out of the ranch yard and headed back up the Hartsock Grade and back towards the colony once more.

Will saddled horses for he and Jeannie and rode with the outgoing crew until they reached the crest of the Hartsock Grade where they stopped and waved the wagons by on their way west... back to the colony expecting them in about five days' time...

Chapter XI
The Plan

It was late and the single dim light bulb powered by the simple DC generator created from the electrical system from a wrecked car and powered by the irrigation ditch that passed by the Quonsets was doing a  poor job of illuminating the tiny corner room the committee had commandeered for this meeting. The setting was austere and the mood somber, but each person in attendance was vitally interested in the outcome of this meeting. Indeed, it seemed the survival of the colony... and of mankind itself might well rest on the decisions made in this conference. While it was entirely true that this committee could not and would not make any binding decisions, they were charged with devising and formulating a plan of action that might both be acceptable to the society as a whole and still achieve the goals of the colony. In essence, they must find the best way open to them to survive!

It had been four days since the scout team had radioed that they were departing the valley of the Tucannon and given the extra day spent in the former town of Walla Walla, they should be arriving sometime tomorrow afternoon. In the time since the scout team had left their midst, there had been much that had happened here. Although it appeared that the marauding gangs were becoming fewer in number, their violence and desperation were increasing. As available food and other supplies dwindled, these groups became more cannibalistic and attacks on one another became more widespread and deadly. Conditions here were rapidly deteriorating into chaos and the committee was convinced that the time to abandon this redoubt was imminent. It had served its purpose, but it was becoming untenable. It was taking more and more of their resources to protect the colony against attack and predation. This winter promised to be long and cold as food became just a memory and shelter even more unfamiliar. Somehow, they had to create a system that would survive.

Mower

The scout team had radioed in from Walla Walla that they had found a boon in equipment there. The Ft. Walla Walla Museum had a rather complete collection of horse drawn implements that could be removed to the new settlement on the river. They had reported plows, disks, mowers, rakes and even a horse drawn potato digger in the museum complex. The buildings were pretty much demolished, but it didn't seem the implements were suffering a similar fate. No action was deemed necessary at present, but note was made and whatever might be needed in the river colony could be relocated then.

After nearly five straight hours of discussion, argument and more discussion, the committee finally decided on a general plan of action to present to the Committee of the Whole in the ensuing morning. Basically,  the plan called for an immediate dispatch of a team of builders to the river location where they would begin with the refurbishment and reconstruction of existing facilities. When this was complete, or as soon as people could be released from that project pending its completion, new buildings were to be completed to be used as homes for the incoming colonists. The committee decided, tentatively, that a crew of about thirty people would be sufficient for this project and would not over task the available resources in the valley. It was decided that this need not be limited to unattached people nor should children be excluded. There would be a real call for people to salvage lumber from the destroyed structures in order to construct new homes and outbuildings. Children were quite capable of much of this work and their help would free others for more technical tasks.

It was further recommended that a teacher be sent along with this vanguard to keep the children's education apace. It was felt that this would be the area of greatest resistance from those who opposed any of the children working if their education was not addressed. It amazed most of the members of this committee that there were still some people in the colony that fought the concept of children being used as part of the workforce that sustained the population. There were myriad jobs that fit their abilities and temperaments. Those in charge of these evolutions were very careful not to overdo any child and their hours of schooling were mandatory, but the simple fact was, they could do jobs that allowed the adults the freedom to tackle the more difficult, dangerous or age appropriate. Some of these people did not seem to understand that this colony was in a fight for survival and most of the niceties of civilization were gone. Life had been reduced to the here and now for the most part and the future was little more than a dream on the far horizon.

As the meeting of the Committee of the Whole began at 0930 the following morning, Jared was amazed to see how heavily the population  had shifted to the predominantly female side. The overall population had increased by what seemed to be about fifty or sixty people and nearly all of the increase was female. When he inquired about this of the group leaders, he was told of a rescue that had taken place on the north side of the Columbia River a few days prior.

It had been the wish of the colony to find some way across the river that did not involve the entire population swimming the flood. Within a reasonable distance of their Kennewick location there were four bridges spanning the river prior to the blast. Three, the Blue Bridge, the Cable Bridge and the railroad bridge were in Kennewick. The fourth, the Interstate Highway Bridge was in Richland... or,

151

rather, they were before the blast. None of the three highway bridges survived and the railroad bridge, a mid-span draw bridge, was stuck in the "up" position. Loss of power had rendered the bridge inoperable and as useless as a rubber nail. Inspection by an engineer lately added to the group, Cynthia Pryor, had yielded the reason for the dilemma. She had explained to the council that the loss of power had activated the "fail-safe" mode of braking much the same as in a modern elevator. There had been a requirement for hydraulic power to hold the brakes open and loss of that had caused them to simply close. She had reasoned that simply relieving the hydraulic lock would allow the span to drop back into its  "down" position. She went on to explain that while it would, likely, close, it would do so without restraint and at the full velocity that gravity could generate.

"In a nutshell," she explained, "it will close, but it may well not be useable or it may even continue down into the river!"

The consensus was that it was not at all usable now, so about anything would have to be an improvement and the mere possibility that it would be useable was a desire worth pursuing. Certainly, it would be no worse than it was now. Obviously, the structure of the bridge was far superior to that of any of the three highway bridges and Cynthia explained that the comparatively short spans, massive girder support and overall design was for a bridge designed to support massive loads instead of mere automobiles with the occasional truck.

Explaining the theory of how to close the span was, as it turned out, the easy part of the equation. Two days of ball-bursting labor followed that yielded two people in the river and having to be picked out by the rescue boat in place for just that eventuality, two more inundated in hydraulic fluid and one man left with an arm broken and a need to be rescued from a makeshift scaffold high in the structure. After seventeen hours of tedious and very dangerous work, some judicious work with gas cutting torches a shout rang out, "She's FREE!" the span crashed into its lowered position.

Actually, crashed was a bit of a misnomer. To many, the thought was that the entire bridge had collapsed but time was to tell it was only the ringing of steel on steel. The first order was to tend to those injured. It was found that, fortunately, the single broken limb was the only injury of that severity. There were several cases of cuts, scrapes and bruises with which to attend, but other than the ever-present concern over infection in this community with a very limited medical pharmacy, the most long-lasting affects were most likely to be those soaked in the slippery, gooey hydraulic oil. Even those unfortunates, though it was reasoned they probably would not squeak for a good long time, would most likely suffer no ill effects from their misadventure.

The really good news was that, even though it would never again be pronounced sufficiently strong to carry loaded freight cars, it seemed likely that the span would be entirely adequate to pass whatever wagons the colony had. A quick security team meeting had ended with a security squad manning positions at each end of the span with orders to control traffic and defend the bridge vehemently.

It was thought that the near explosive level of sound generated would attract most all remaining inhabitants of the areas... a supposition not to go unfulfilled, certainly. Most of the colony knew what was about and were not alarmed to hear the crash but those not in this group had no such warning. Soon there were small bands of people lurking about in the shadows of the team still working on the site. The security squads were still in view, so there was no overt challenge from any of these groups though it was feared they might be tested after nightfall.

It was late in the day and darkness was rapidly approaching when a shot rang out from the rubble north of the bridge in the area where the Port of Pasco complex used to stand. That shot was

Port Facility

followed closely by another and a scream of someone in pain. The security detail at the north end of the bridge immediately deployed to protect the bridge aprons and deny crossing to dangerous elements. Within a few minutes, a small band of people was spotted making their way towards the bridge. Since, other than the port facility, there was no other structure in immediate sight, the team had a good field of vision across the gray expanse and each watched

154

diligently in their assigned area. Soon it became apparent that those people were attempting to elude others and were being as furtive as a group of people can be.

That this was a group consisting of mainly women with a few children became evident when they emerged from the last bit of cover. As they moved toward the bridge apron suddenly a shout rang out and a gang of thugs broke out of the ruins of the houses across Ainsworth Street and gave chase to the now fleeing women. From the top of the bridge framework shots rang out... not meant to kill those shooting across the way but to get them to go to ground so the fleeing women could make their escape. No one on that bridge knew what was happening on the ground there, but it was fairly obvious that thugs were chasing women and in that race, most would bet on the women any time!

The sound of gunfire from the bridge startled the fleeing women and they stopped dead in their tracks. Instantly, two of the security force at ground level on the bridge apron stood and called to the women to come on quickly. They shouted that they were bridge guards from the Columbia Colony and would cover their escape if they would hurry. Tentatively at first and then more quickly, the escaping gang began moving toward the bridge and seeming safety. None but knew they may well be moving into a situation as bad as or, possibly, worse than that they had just escaped, but, somehow, the anxiety carried in that guard's voice did not create an aura of danger. As one, they hurried on towards the span. Once again, the band of thugs, seeing their quarry escaping let out a rousing battle yell and charged on toward the bridge.

Their leader had assumed that those shots had come from one or two armed dudes who wanted to play Rambo... well, he thought, he knew how to play this game a bit himself and he surmised that if he and his gang held this bridge, they could charge anything they wanted to cross it and the mutts would have to pay up or swim for it! It is probably apros pos that the young thug never knew the fallacy in his thinking for he had not covered ten feet when four fully automatic AR-15s opened up and the leading edge of his attacking force melted like the cheese on an overheated pizza. Pablo was the first to die on that railroad track leading to the bridge, but he was not the last, certainly for in the space of thirty-five seconds three of his companions shared his fate and the rest were running as hard as they could back to the ruins they had so recently left behind. As soon as the escaping women were beyond the defense line on the bridge, they slowed but there were, instantly, those there to hurry them onward across the bridge and to safety. It was soon enough that the cluster found their way to the safety of the south bank of the great river and into the arms of people there who could help them on their way.

In a matter of several more minutes, wagons had delivered the frightened, hungry, beaten and defiant group to the colony site. The leader of the group stepped forward. From the group that had assembled in front of the Quonsets to see what was under way, a female voice rang out. "That's Ilya! She was the leader of the Cruz Azul gang that attacked this place before."

Before the girl could move, strong hands grabbed her and held her firmly. She did not struggle with her captor, but stood stoically and waited for the tumult to calm. When order had descended on the group, the leader was taken to a table at one corner of the compound and Andy Kane himself stepped forth to speak to her.

Without comment, Ilya waited patiently while Andy consulted with the young red-head she had believed unable to speak who they had simply called Jane Doe. Obviously she was doing a great deal better as she no longer looked like a walking skeleton with piercings and hollow, haunted eyes. There was a young man hovering close beside her who Ilya thought she recognized as one from that old group too. She could not rightly remember what had happened to this pair. She had assumed that everyone who had attacked that day had died there on that tarmac in front of those sheds. Obviously, at least two had not. Also, just as obviously, it would have been safer for her if there had been no survivors of the CA-13 gang but that was not the case and she would just have to deal with it. The first thing the woman did was to acknowledge the young woman with a smile and a greeting. When her mention of "Jane" was quickly countermanded by "Arlene", Ilya stated how pleased she was that Arlene had recovered from her trauma. The Russian woman then made a decision that no gang member would ever make, and she hoped fervently that this rather official looking man doing the interviewing would realize that to be the case. She spoke to him directly without being asked. "Sir, what Arlene has said is the truth. There are two of us here who are survivors of that gang. My mate, Shar Lewis is also here. May I call her forward too?"

Andy was having trouble following her heavily accented English but caught the gist of what she was saying,

157

though he wasn't sure if her use of the word "mate" meant the same thing to her as it did to him but he nodded to her to indicate she should do just that.

Ilya turned to the clustered group and motioned for Shar to join her at the inquisition table. As the woman walked forward, the looks exchanged by the two women told Andy that he was not mistaken... that her use of the word, indeed, did have the same connotation he'd assigned it. The dark-haired woman moved to a position beside her friend and nodded to Arlene to indicate that she did remember her. She then turned to Col. Kane and said, "Sir, we have no weapons, but if you need to be sure of that, you may, of course search us. It's quite true we were part of that gang but pulled out of it before that lousy attack went down. We tried to abort the whole thing, but we could not stop the headstrong. Since then, we have been living pretty much by our wits until we became part of a small colony over near where the airport was in Pasco. We were captured from there when the camp was overrun by the gang you saw pursuing us. They had pretty much killed all the men and had herded all of us women into a pen to hold until they could break us later when Ilya and I figured out a way to escape. The problem came when we realized we had all these women to bring with us... Well," she said with a note of frustration, "we couldn't leave them there to the whims of that bunch. Those are some mean dudes in that gang."

Ilya took up the narrative there and described how they had waited until the gang had moved them to the old Port Facility because there was a semi-intact Quonset there that would serve to hold us. "We had just been moved to the spot when there was that huge sound from the bridge and someone said the span had been lowered. We had crossed it to get to the Pasco side by climbing on top of the girders until we got on the far side of the raised part. Anyway, when that clang rang out, and they knew the

Columbia River

bridge was down, they called all their brothers together and were making plans to charge it and take control of it. We didn't wait to plan, while they were talking and arguing, Shar and I urged the women to their feet and we ran for it. We figured that anyone who could do that to the bridge had to have a lot more sense than this rabble who had us and even not knowing what we were getting into, we thought it had to be better than what we were leaving for no one didn't know what they meant to do with us."

"Whatever you plan to do to us," Shar stated, "these other women didn't have nothing to do with what Ilya and I may have been part of, if you understand me."

Andy dismissed the two women to return to their group and to join them in getting cleaned up and being fed while he took the issue up with the Executive Council. The Council heard from Gabe and Arlene as to what had happened in that CA-13 gang and what they knew about the attack on the compound. When both of the young people admitted that neither of these women had ever been mean or vicious to anyone except in defense of the group and that the actual attack on this compound had been the idea of the two

159

Mexican brothers and Rob, the committee, after deliberation, decided to admit the pair on probation to the colony. It was decided that, for the time being, their presence on any group that required them to go armed would not happen.

Andy called the women back to his area and explained what had been decided and asked if that was something they could accept, or would they rather move on and continue living on their own.

"Colonel," Shar began after a quick look at her mate for acceptance, "we were not doing so well on our own. We understand your need for this probation period so we will accept whatever restrictions you impose on us. Our only concern is that... well, to be blunt, we're a couple and I know most of the people A Couple here are from various church groups, especially the Mormons as they were about the only ones prepared at all to meet a disaster like this. Will our sexuality cause problems in the group?"

Andy smiled softly and stated, "Before this started, perhaps so, but if these people have learned anything since it's that to have survived is such a blessing that old standards of morality do not apply. Today we have to live under a much more socially diverse set of rules... the first of which is that there aren't many rules that apply. Today we

160

have survivors of all races, creeds colors and sexual orientations living in our group. It may come down to the point that all may be asked to parent children in order to sufficiently span the gene pool. Any such request would come from the Committee officially, if necessary, so we are addressing that contingency with all new members. We don't have any method yet of Artificial Insemination, so if it ever comes to it, it would have to be done the old fashioned way to insure genetic diversity. I can promise you will not be high on the list to be asked unless you request it. So... there it is in a nutshell, can you accept us on those terms?"

Ilya and Shar looked at one another and grinned. Ilya responded first. "Colonel, neither of us was exclusively gay before we met, so, no, that would not be a problem for us. We have talked about how we might someday have a family and I think with that thought in mind, you might put our names on that list right now."

When Andy turned his head to the other woman, she responded with a quick nod of her head and an affirmation that she too felt this way.

Thusly, were the two former gang members admitted to the colony and no one knew the joy the women felt on the inside, but the grin on the outside served notice they were happy to be here. At once the pair made themselves useful to the colony as a whole and spoke openly of all they had endured to survive to the point they had now reached. Time would tell for this couple, but there were many who accepted them without reservation, a few who had doubts and a handful that was openly hostile... or would have been had the rest of the colony permitted it.

Inside, while the new assimilations were being processed, another meeting of the Executive Council was in session. There was a specific agenda for today's meeting. To that end, Rae Lynn and Adam Stuart were addressing the committee.

"The facts are," Rae Lynn stated, "we have become a young and decidedly female camp. We are now numbered, with all the latest additions added, two hundred and fifty-nine souls above the age of fourteen years. There are only ten of these over age fifty-five and one hundred sixty are female, only ninety-nine male. This is an over three to two female to male ratio. We also have some gay couples so Ilya and Shar are by no means unique. It seems that the latter finds tend to trend more to that dimension... especially among the females. In short, we are a microcosm of society before the devastation and it appears that we will remain so. Our present problem is, very simply stated, we have many more women than we do men. That is the bad news. The good news is that with a bit of care in selection of mates, we can effectively generate a strong genetic cross section with just those in camp now. There will need to be a registry of sorts in place for future generations so that mates are chosen with these features in mind. I have a call out for anyone with training in that area to come forth to direct our efforts. To address the problem of three women for each two men, however, will require a bit more than a registry."

At the mention of this problem, Mrs. Carrington, the matriarch of an old and historic family in the area spoke up directly. "Young lady, please do not insult us by suggesting that it would be proper to have more than one

162

wife. The Bible EXPRESSLY forbids and condemns such practices and I will certainly not allow it here!"

As the chair gaveled for order, Rae Lynn continued, "Mrs. Carrington, with all due respect, how many wives did Abraham have? Wasn't it old Israel that married the sisters Rachael and Leah? To say that the Bible forbids multiple wives is simply not true. Further, may I remind you that we

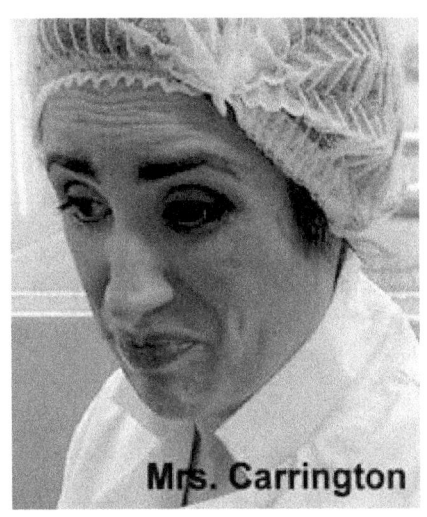

Mrs. Carrington

have zero authority to tell anyone how they must live their lives at this point. There simply are no laws nor, if there were, anyone to enforce them nor stop violators. Our philosophy to date has simply been to make sure that actions do not hurt the community as a whole, affect its health or endanger its occupants. Beyond that, all we can do is turn them out. We have no morality police and nothing that people do within the walls of their own home, as it were, is of any concern to any other person. We are conducting our church services in a very generic way so as to exclude no one. We even have Jewish people holding services, but we cannot, nor should we command people to believe this way or that. If you cannot accept the will of the majority on this issue, there is nothing that forces you to stay here and live with the situation as it is. We would not put you out as long as you are not disruptive, nor will anyone be allowed to put you into that position where you would have to participate in the practice. That said, what say you?"

The woman frowned deeply for a moment, hating the fact that she was forced into this corner by this snippy young woman when she realized the young woman was correct in everything she had said. Plural marriage was a precept of the Old Testament and she had forgotten that. No one was making her join in the practice and they really didn't have the right to tell others what to do in their own lives so she sighed and said... "Of course you are right, Mrs. Stuart. Times have changed and we truly are in a survival mode, aren't we. I suppose it will be the spawn of many new or the revival of old concepts. It will be our chore to keep up, I suppose."

"Well said, Mrs. Carrington," said the committee chairman. "It is indeed a time of adaptations. I hope you can continue to teach us the object lessons we need to learn."

With everything on the committee's agenda complete save the last, the mood turned serious as they took up the need to select the advance team members that will be moving out to new settlement on the Tucannon. To this end, a survey had been made of the colony and all of those with talents in the building trades were placed on a master list. The committee was pleased to see that there were a number of women on the list. The biggest fear they had as a group was that severe inroads would be made into the male population of the colony remaining through the winter that might make their security vulnerable. Without a doubt, they had women on the security team but the heart of that team was the males.

The resident engineer, Cynthia Pryor, was placed in overall charge of the construction project. Her charge was to have habitation ready by the middle of April for two hundred and seventy-five people. Most of it was already there and needed only cleaning and rehabilitation for the new tenants. As the conversation ebbed and flowed, a sudden idea popped into the woman's fertile mind.

"I wonder," she began quietly, "if we could repurpose one of those hundreds of wind turbines to our purposes? There is, after all, little real difference between using wind to power the device and using water. Just one of those could provide adequate power for our entire community on the river." For just a few moments she contemplated the situation then she continued. "Could you assign me one more stout wagons and five more stout people? I will put a small team to that task. We have a couple of very capable electricians in our band who could very easily handle the technical aspects."

When the objection was raised that they were all blown down in the blast, she simply stated that merely being blown over would not harm anything beyond the tower, the blade and the nacelle, none of which were important in what she was contemplating. When she went on to explain the

165

rudiments of her plan and to explain the benefits that could be gained from it, the committee quickly authorized placing the concept before the Committee of the Whole for their consideration.

It was a cold, crisp morning in early November when the construction team rolled out of the colony yard on their way to a destiny unknown. Ten freight wagons carrying almost twenty tons of supplies that ranged from food to tools to reclaimed building supplies led the procession across the black bridge that marked the beginning of their trek. On these wagons rode the drivers. The people on this trek ranged in age from ten years to nearly fifty. The remaining fifteen or so mounted members of the party rode independently as outriders and guards while the rest walked. Those walking switched off with the riders regularly so no one felt burdened. One addition to this party that had not existed on the previous trek was a lightweight, versatile wagon whose only purpose was as a cook

Chuckwagon

shed. At Lila's suggestion and urging, the Charlie Goodnight invention of the chuckwagon had been reborn. Flanking this train to the edge of the danger zone was a strong contingent of the Colony Defense Committee.

The feeling that they had not seen the last of that vicious gang from which they had plucked the last group of refugee women was strong and it was felt that an

166

overwhelming military presence was the best deterrent to further depredations by this gang. The day was just fully light when this protective force watched the train disappear over a low rise on their way up the Snake River, roughly following the route run previously by the scout troupe.

The plan was for the chuckwagon, light and fast as it was, to make all speed to a point forward on the trail where Lila and her cook team would set up their camp and get their meal preparations underway. The noon meal was, of course, the major meal of the day for the troupe, so it required the most planning and time for preparation.

Dutch Oven Biscuits

The first day's nooning was to be in the vicinity of the railroad crossing where the old asparagus shed and packing house was located. Lila was interested in seeing if the freezing unit they had found on the prior trip was still operating and if she could utilize anything from within the industrial sized freezers found there. As soon as the cooks arrived, Lila gave instructions for setting up the wagon, arranging the items to be prepared and lighting the fires they'd need for preparing the meal. The first meal out would be quick and easy as they had brought the fixings with them from the colony, knowing how short time would be this first time.

Lila was disappointed to find that the freezer unit was no longer operating, having run itself out of fuel in the interim since she was last here, but she was highly impressed with the speed and ease with which her team had prepared a very hearty and tasty meal for those following. The team had just finished their own meals when a shout rang out from the lookout that the train was in view and would be arriving within the hour. It was fortunate that in this location on the crest of a small rise, the view behind them on the trail was unobstructed. That this would not always be so was apparent which caused the head cook to suggest to the wagon captain, Bart Roberts, that when he was within an hour of the projected camp that he should send ahead a pair of runners to announce the imminent arrival of the train. This would be a way of affording the cooks the opportunity to finish the last minute preparations and have the meals

Dutch Oven Bread

ready to serve immediately on arrival of the hungry crew. Probably the major benefit of this would be that the cook crew would then be able to clean their gear and stow it while the meal was being completed, allowing them to push off as soon as their cook gear was stowed. Each crewman was responsible for his own personal eating gear so "doing the dishes" was not a responsibility of the cooks.

In this case, the potato sheds at Eureka Flats would be the site of the evening camp. Although this was not that far along the way, it was situated at the top of the steepest upgrade of the entire journey. Bart felt that his teams would be very jaded after completing that pull and, as they were not on any time table to complete this trek, they could use the extra time to recruit their stock.

Days here were short at this time of year so travel time was greatly limited and as cold as it was, it was a thoroughly chilled group that enjoyed the light repast the cook crew had ready for them. For the cooks, this was the busiest time of the day. The fry bread and Dutch oven biscuits needed for tomorrow's meals were made now. There was time for leavening to have its effect on the doughs and the baking time would not slow their travel. Cooking with a Dutch oven is an art and Lila was well versed in the intricacies of that art. Her offerings were both delicious and hearty. She kept her crew well fed, well-nourished and coming back for more. There was not an easy way to provide food for that many people. Lila had to plan closely and training her people was an essential part of what she was doing. It was well enough that she knew how to go about her tasks, but it was essential that she made sure her apprentices did as well, for she could not be at every camp in the river valley and it would be necessary to have many separate mess sites available to them. Besides, she thought, it would be nice to have a bit of time to herself with her mates, Will and Jeannie.

The trip was not without incident, nor was it without toil, but four days later it was a very excited Bart and Stella Roberts who leaped down off their wagon seat to greet the Baylor family at their remote ranch. He first introduced his chief engineer, Cynthia Pryor and then got out of the way when an excited head cook came barreling out to welcome all to her Tucannon River Camp...

169

Chapter XII
River Camp

As soon as Bud DeWitt heard his twin, Eric, was back he used it as an excuse to ask for relief from his duties at the McDowell place and return to be with his brother. Actually, he reasoned, the ranch here was in good hands. Even Kayla had returned when the baby perked up on a new regimen and was growing strong and healthy. Sary's twin siblings, Ian and Ann were helping Justin with the livestock and doing quite well, though they obviously missed their parents terribly.

To compensate for the move of Bud from the ranch, it was decided to send some help. Volunteers were called for and three were chosen. Aaron Smoot was a resourceful young man of about twenty-seven years. When Aaron was picked, twenty-four year old Stefanie Bailey immediately volunteered as did Stef's younger sister, LeAnne. Care was taken to explain the duties expected from this relief team and they were sent on their way with time enough to make the change before nightfall.

It took no time at all for the trio to fit in on the ranch. Aaron and Justin worked seamlessly and Stef did all she could to learn the routine as quickly as possible. She was not happy working in the house with the children whereas LeAnne loved helping Sary run the house. Together they kept a very neat home and the baby prospered in their care.

The twins, Ian and Ann were inseparable in all things. They spent most of their day either doing their assigned school lessons or helping Justin and Aaron with the animals. The thing they liked best were the rabbits and they could spend hours tending them. They were less than thrilled when it came time to butcher, but a serious talk  from Sary and LeAnne convinced them it was essential and they consented to the need and, eventually, they even didn't mind participating in the chore.

The Eric 'n Bud reunion was quick, short and boisterous! As soon as the dust settled, it was announced that the four of them, the twins plus Kayla and Jenna, would be setting out at first light for the Andersson place and if needed, to look for them there. It was decided that, for the time, at least, a radio would not be needed as there was little construction to be done just now and they could clean up without need for constant communication.

Sunup found the four hiking up the old roadway that led to their creek. It was a fair hike and a wagon full of necessary items would be along shortly but in the meantime, the team decided to make sure their water supply was good, dig a hole for a latrine and get something on to eat. While Eric dug out a shovel and started making ready to do battle with the ash and earth, his new wife came forth and said, "Darling, why are you starting a new hole? Don't you realize all of these outlying ranches had outhouses that they used regularly?"

Kayla had to laugh at the man's confused expression as it dawned on him what that meant and he laughed inside as put his tools back and started a thorough search of the ranch yard. His little faux pas as pointed out by his bride served as a wakeup call and he decided a full inventory of what was already here might well be in order. He yelled out for Bud, but Kayla immediately hushed him as she told him that Bud and Jenna were in the poultry barns making sure everything was in working order there and she was quite sure Jenna did not want her time with Eric's twin interrupted for anything less than an emergency. Eric smiled knowingly as he nodded his head slowly. "If you need help," Kayla continued, the cleanup work inside the house can be delayed some."

"No," Eric said after a moment's consideration. "I think I can handle this on my own then I'll be in to help you. Please don't lift anything heavy. Call for me or wait until I'm free and I will be happy to help you with whatever you need."

The work went quickly for the team. Kayla and Eric found as many excuses as they could imagine to find time to come together. Sometimes they would hold one another and kiss deeply... at others it was just a touch of the finger tips but, at all times, the touches were electric. The attractive blonde lady found her heart melting when this tall, strong man came near her. She did not know where these feelings were coming from as her original marriage had not included such feelings. Oh, it was not without love. Her man was quite kind and nice and he treated her like a queen. It was on a sudden thought that she realized... Eric does not treat her like a queen. She is on no pedestal in his mind. The thought was a bit shocking as it came to her, but she realized this truth. To Eric she was not a queen... nor was she an adored, untouchable marble statue. No... to Eric, she was a woman. She was his mate... his partner... his equal!

Suddenly she understood, she didn't like being someone's queen, she loved being a man's woman! His loving partner... his mate. It was so important now to understand that they were a team. It was the Eric and Kayla Team with the capital T in its proper place. She was here because he wanted her here not because she was a centerfold quality beauty. She was not some hothouse flower a man would be afraid to pick. She was a woman to walk beside her man and she loved that not only had she realized this for herself, but that her chosen man and understood it instinctively.

For the first time since that stupid rock had slammed into them causing the destruction of life as it had long been, she understood they were going to survive. They were going to have children and they were going to begin to repopulate the world. It would be alright... she now knew that. Life would go on. Oh my how wonderful was that thought in her mind.

Now her mind went to Jenna and the things that were important in that girl's mind, for it was these children who were important. What should she be teaching the young woman? What was important for her to know? Certainly the earth and its population had no reason to return to the way it was. There was reason to squabble over neither global warming nor a diminishing supply of petroleum in the world. It mattered not right now. There was nothing to burn those fuels even if they existed... not in a quantity, at least, to create a level of  concern. Right now, all that was certain was that there was junk falling from the sky and who knew when it would stop.

Excitedly, Kayla started towards the barn with the intention of sharing what she knew with her very attractive niece. As she opened the door to the rabbit barn, she heard and saw nothing so she moved on through the poultry sections, both immaculately tended. When she opened the door to the goat barn, she heard voices but she said nothing, lost as she was in her own revelations... she moved with a care learned as a result of some inner knowledge that told her a wound today could well be the end of her tomorrow. In so doing, she happened on the two, Bud and Jenna, as they sat on upturned buckets talking quietly while their heads were touching. Each held the other's hands and quietly they communed. The scene was beyond touching as Kayla brought herself to a full stop and just stared at the

174

vision before her. As she watched, a voice came into her mind...

"Kayla," the voice intoned, *"leave these be. It is important to us that they become one as they have a great and important part to play in the near future. Afford them this time to bond and become as one even as you and your man have done. There is special works being wrought here."*

Without speaking aloud, the woman nodded her head and thought, I know what he says is true but where will all this end? Almost at once, a vision opened before her showing a verdant and abundant world. Trees were in profusion and crops tall and green to the horizon. Overhead, a brilliant sun shone down from a crystal clear azure sky and birds winged their way to and fro. In her mind's eye, she could see a world such as did not exist around her now. Today all was the gray of volcanic ash ripped from a thousand mountain tops from Tierra del Fuego to the tip of the Aleutian Chain and sent on winds around the world.  Here and there were tiny oases of life, but, for the most part, the earth had ceased to sustain her children. Very little lived in this devastated land. Nothing survived that needed sustenance from green and growing things for there were nonesuch in the land. These people existed simply because they had been very, very lucky and some few had heeded advice and had created an emergency supply which had sustained them until now.

For the first time in the seeming age since this began, these few people were beginning to renew themselves. Survival was not ensured, certainly, and existence was tenuous at best, but steps were being taken. Here, today, four people had established not only contact, but a rapport with an primal species that, had you polled the colony at the potato sheds, would have told one they did not even exist. Such was life. It persevered. Beyond all odds, it lived.

If nine of ten species then in existence had perished in totality when this event happened so many millennia before then, certainly, the destruction was even worse today. There were no humans alive sixty five million years ago at the end of the cretaceous period but if there had been, most likely they would not be here today.

Kenorah

"Kayla," the voice continued, *"what know you of healing? How learned are you in the selection of herbs to help one overcome illness and injury?"*

"I know but very little," she said, audibly. "I know that Jeannie has some knowledge in that area, but it is not substantial. Why do you ask, Sir?"

"My name is Kenorah, you may address me with that, if you wish," he said as he continued. *"Within our clan, we have some very good*

176

healers. They are well versed in these arts. It is, after all, how we must treat ourselves. It is not our desire at this time to draw more into our group than those here. Does no one here have a desire to learn?"

"I do!" came a shout from the barns. In a moment's time, Jenna burst out the front door and exclaimed, "I have been learning some with Mama and I'd love to know more. Could I do this for us?"

"I think you would be a good person to begin with," the voice continued. "We shall begin your education as soon as you have done all you need here to put things in order."

"Do I have time for a honeymoon too before we begin?" the girl asked with a slight giggle.

"What is this 'honeymoon' of which you speak? ... Ah... I see what you are asking. Can you forego that for now and take it up when your training is further along?"

"I can, Kenorah," the girl responded. I was not serious about traveling now anyway and I know we are well needed here where we are presently. I will be ready when you call."

"That is proper," the large fellow answered into her mind. "Please know, young one, that the work you do here is very highly appreciated by my people. We have been in touch with other remnants and we are finding we are lucky. We are bringing more to us as we find them living and can do what is necessary. There are not many, but here and yon, there are a few of us still living. I think we need to consolidate our population for now until we can maintain a viable breeding population. In-breeding is ever a concern

177

with us because never is our population high and care must always be taken to preclude the possibility of breeding too closely. For this reason, before this situation, we traveled very far to take a mate. It was not at all uncommon for one to travel from here in the far western lands to the midlands or even to the great sea in the east to find a mate."

"Wow," an amazed Kayla stated, "that is very special, but how would one from here know that one there would be willing? I can assume you could talk to one another as you are now talking to us, but was that enough?"

"No, it is not," the voice replied. "As a group, as a species, we have regular regional meetings. From here we often traveled to what you call Alberta, Canada or to the dry lands of Nevada or even Arizona to meet. It was at these meetings where matings were proposed and joinings accepted. It is normal that from this point, the female would travel to the male's home to meet his family and for them to decide if a mating between them would be proper and tenable for it is seldom that such a mating is set aside. Once the mating is decided upon, the couple would then journey to the female's clan where they would normally make their home. Rarely, and that is usually in the case where the mating male is a leader in his clan or is otherwise very necessary to his clan, the couple will stay with the male's clan. Our matings, like yours, are designed for life and unless something happens that would interrupt that life, it is so."

It was Jenna who then asked, *"Kenora, we have not yet seen you. Is there a reason for that?"*

178

"There is," the large one said. "I am very large and I do not look like you. We have been portrayed as monsters for many millennia and we would not want to frighten you. It is essential that we establish a working relationship with you and with your people. We would not wish the situation to recur where we are not known and people either fear us or do not believe in our existence. You should have no trouble remembering the situation in the world just prior to this calamity striking. There was virtual war in the world of 'research' concerning us. There were those who saw us as a kind of ape and others who revered us as Gods. Neither are, of course true, but it was impossible to make real headway in this field under those conditions. The separate factions had barricaded themselves, intellectually at least, into their camps and they would verbally and, in some cases, physically assail anyone that did not share their viewpoint. 'Don't drink the Kool-aid' was a battle cry for many of these people. We simply could not work with those conditions prevailing.

We had worked very hard to get the information out to different groups with information of our true nature, but it all became impossible to pursue. We had very brave members of our species that made themselves available for contact. It happened in the area you call California when a young male left his calling card around some of the equipment used to move earth so your machines that carry you could get into the remote places. Many tracks were left and much other evidence and what happened?"

"I know what happened," Eric answered when the others did not. "The owner of the construction crew made fake feet and paraded around to negate the finding you had

179

left for them. The newspaper in Eureka had come to the site and had done an excellent article on the tracks found. Even Dr. Ivan Sanderson became involved and wrote many magazine articles and some books about your people that were fact filled and very interesting. But, a skeptical news media chose to report the fact that Wallace had made fake tracks and did all they could to make a joke of the situation. That atmosphere still prevailed up until this disaster occurred."

"Never once did they stop to investigate why Wallace would do such a thing," Eric continued, "The simple fact was, these road builders were working out of a camp in the remote woods. They lived and worked on the roads all week and returned to their homes in town only on the weekends. When those tracks appeared around Jerry Crew's cat, many men quit and would not return to the job out of fear. Ray Wallace simply could not keep a crew so he perpetrated that hoax to be able to say, 'Oh, it was just me, playing around.' When, in fact, he was in far off Costa Rica on the twenty-fifth of August in 1958 when those tracks appeared. He did not return to the jobsite in California until after the first of October, 1958. It would certainly be amazing if he had been able to create fake tracks in the loose dirt on his job from thousands of miles away in Central America!"

"That is true," Kenorah stated. *"We saw almost immediately that this would not be sufficient, so we had a young woman volunteer to let herself be filmed. Almost a decade after that attempt to contact people in that basin, we tried again with a different scenario. We were in contact with an avid fan of our people. He was determined to find enough evidence to make a film that he might prove to the world that we really are viable people. We returned to this same area and waited until the conditions were just perfect before she showed herself to the pair who were riding on the backs of the large animals you call horses. This young woman was very brave to do this and she performed this over the protests of many of our people."*

"It should be remembered that many of our number were not in favor of any part of this evolution. They are not friendly to your type of person at all as they have suffered many indignities at their hands and would rather we just retreated from your type and not have anything to do with you.

Freeman Female

We cannot do that, however, as there are extreme dangers inherent in the ways you do things. Undoubtedly, that situation was altered by that huge rock striking our earth and we are now in a desperate struggle, along with you, for our survival."

Paul Freeman with Hand Cast of a Bigfoot taken from Upper Dry Creek above Dixie, WA. April 21, 1994

"After that film was released, the results were not much different from what had gone on before. We were quite shocked as a people to learn that your society was not going to be accepting of us in any form except, perhaps, as an exhibit in one or you caged places where animals are kept for seeing. More attempts were made to provide film. Another lady showed herself to a man very near where we are right now about twenty years past. She was carrying her baby and had her young one, about seven years old, in the brush waiting for her. It was a very dangerous thing to do, but we had been watching this Freeman person for some time and felt we could trust him with our woman and children. He tried very hard to get this film before the people of your nation, but the derision was terrible to behold and we were very much upset by what happened to him. He did no more than we had him do and your people who tell the news did terrible things to him. He answered them honestly and they made much fun of him and treated him like he was a trickster. It was most sad to us."

"At this time, it was decided that this direction would not work. We had been working for generations with various people at different levels of understanding and we consulted them. We learned that it would probably never come to pass through the medium of photography or audio recordings in and of themselves. We even provided samples of our language to people who knew what constituted language and still it was not enough."

182

When Kayla looked askance at this statement, Eric went on to explain how Al Barry and Ron Morehead had recorded many conversations from their hunting camp in the Sierra Nevada near Lake Tahoe in California. A retired cryptolinguist with over twenty years' experience in the US Navy heard these tapes and realized immediately that they were a form of language. "You must understand," Eric stated to the other three with him, "the job of a cryptolinguist is to listen to voices and determine if what he is hearing is language or mere gibberish. Even though he may not speak the language to which he was listening, he had to be able to recognize it and send it on to those who do speak that particular language."

"That's amazing," Jenna stated with eyes wide. "How ever would he know what is real speech in a language he doesn't understand?"

"I'm not sure," Eric answered, "but it has something to do with the morphemes or syllables that make up the word. I guess it's that and a ton of experience doing it. I know that the people who do that are usually found somewhere just listening to radio traffic and learning what they can."

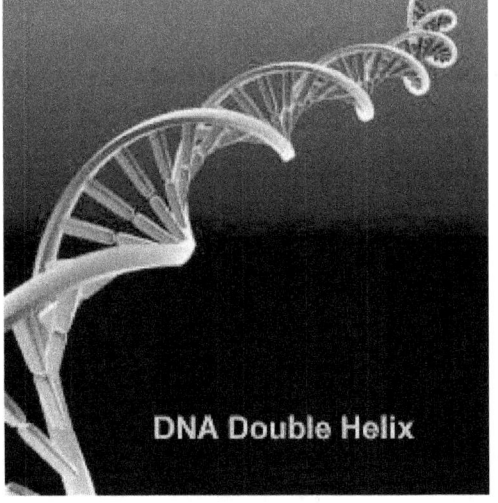

DNA Double Helix

"When it had become obvious to us that the overall public was so difficult to

183

convince, we decided more drastic measures were needed. We worked through some dedicated people and, knowing that human technology had reached a point where DNA research was proving interesting. We did not know what it would take to effect this but we started out by leaving hair in obvious places. Once, in Canada, one of our people stepped where he should not and left a lot of his blood on a board that was designed to keep bears from approaching a fishing cabin when the owners were away. It was something new to him and he hurt himself badly enough he needed a good deal of care to recover from this mistake."

"Our first efforts were not very successful since our DNA is too similar to yours and the samples we provided were just said to have been contaminated by those collecting the samples. There were tests run in British Columbia, Canada and in Minnesota before a major effort was made to bring it forth in a controlled method. Unfortunately, this effort was no more successful than were the prior attempts. It was not that the samples were bad nor were the procedures faulty... it was simply that people where predisposed against the finding before the results were ever announced. The whole scene deteriorated into a huge shouting match where the principals involved were excoriated by people who knew not the difference between mitochondrial DNA and nuclear DNA, let alone the ramifications that were brought forth in this study."

"We decided at this point that it was useless to pursue this further on a macro level. We decided a paradigm shift in thinking was needed back to the micro level and what it had been prior to the DNA study. It was determined that we would abandon those large schemes and just return

184

to finding individuals with whom we could work and continue as we were... then that rock fell out of the sky and everything is different now."

To this point, Bud had been listening quietly without saying anything. Jenna was sitting in front of him as they listened to this disembodied voice. Finally, he spoke, "I understand all that has gone before. I recall reading where, when Roger Patterson made his film available to the academic types who should have been ecstatic to have the opportunity at a new discovery, many of them refused to even look at the film, saying, 'this creature is a myth, so any film purporting to show him has to be a myth as well...' and they would not even entertain the possibility they could be incorrect. They were so convinced of their own rightness that they would not even admit the possibility that they might not know all knowledge. It's a pity really but it is past. Our chore is to figure out what to do to prevent that from happening again in this new age that is dawning."

The four people who and been chosen and who had chosen this task of guarding the domain of this remnant population of these magnificent beings were deep in thought and were contemplating the importance of that which they and just learned from the voice in their minds when, as one, their eyes lifted and beheld a giant standing before them...

Chapter XIII
Expansion

It was not until late afternoon of a windy April day that the wagon train descended the steep grade at Hartsock into the Valley of the Tucannon. Spirits were high and joy reigned supreme as the two hundred and twenty seven souls looked down into the canyon they would now call home. Although a long and dreary winter had given way to an ash clogged spring, spirits had not followed the mercury as the temperatures again warmed enough to allow this exodus. It had taken this arrival to cause the spirit of indominabilty that is inherently human to appear resurgent in the community.

The sense of loss that that had prevailed since leaving the known environs of the war ravaged city seemed to just dissipate as the settlers watched the once beautiful valley open before them as they  crawled down the steep grade. Most knew this area as it was a favorite outdoor recreation area prior to the advent of the fiery death from above, but few had seen it as it now was, choked in ash and without a green leaf showing. The river still wound its way around the huge rocks as it meandered back and forth across the valley floor, but it appeared now, more dead than alive. It was here that people had been coming for years to fish for trout, salmon and steelhead... it was here they had come to hunt the elk, the moose, the mule deer and in later years, the Rio Grande Turkeys that had been introduced here so successfully. It was here the ill-advised and wholly misinformed perpetrators of the 1847 Whitman Massacre had come to attempt to escape retribution for their deed. Now, today, a new group had come... not to recreate... not to escape justice, but to plant new roots and begin to grow again. They were not the only people left alive in the world for, surely, others had been as lucky somewhere, but that they were among the few they also knew.

In the lead wagon, still bright from being newly made, despite the rigors of the few day long trail trek had imposed on it, carried vital gear. In fact, virtually all the wagons carried gear and not people. People could walk and they did. It took this train but eight days to complete the nearly ninety mile trek to the valley from the confluence of the Snake River with the Columbia River. On this trip, only the old, the very young and the infirm rode, all else walked the easy grades of what once had been Highway 124.

Slowly and carefully, wagon after laden wagon descended into the valley via the winding two mile grade that dropped nearly fifteen hundred feet. This made it steep enough to be interesting and demand that care and caution be used, but not so steep that it was deadly. One wagon, then another... the next and the next again made their winding way to the Promised Land below.

Waiting at the bottom of the grade, anticipating their arrival, Will and a party of the advance team welcomed the newcomers and explained there were temporary accommodations awaiting them just a short drive down the valley. He explained that some large growing sheds had been cleaned out and put to the purpose of housing the new immigrants until they found the spot they wished to settle and homestead. He explained that a good sized party had been putting together a bit of a welcome celebration and he'd lead them on down to the spot.

Within minutes of arriving, the Executive Committee was in session and taking questions from the new settlers. First and foremost on the minds of the group was, "When can we find our place...?" The committee  explained, for the tenth time, it seemed that the first order of business would be to get crops into the ground in the houses that had been built for that reason.

"I know you are all extremely anxious to create some sort of normalcy from all the chaos we've been enduring since that asteroid fell on us," Jared began. "I understand that and I can certainly join you in that wish. The facts are, however, in order to survive, we must insure our own community supplies first and, as time allows, we will begin on each individual's needs. That does not mean you will be ignored. We will not be taking applications of land grants for at least as long as until the crops are in and stored. That certainly does not mean you are not free to explore and search out what suits you best."

"Yeah," a voice from the group called out, "so you guys can hog up all the good places..."

Immediately, a hush fell over the crowd as the speaker turned toward the area from which the voice came. Jared turned to it and started slowly, "If anyone is dissatisfied with the by-laws under which we are incorporated, he is free to leave and return to the city we left. He is also free to depart this valley and find whatever suits his need. It will NOT be in this valley, I assure you for we will be of a mind here or the dissenter will be sent away."

"We mean to survive and that is far from certain at this point. One of the most difficult aspects of communal living as we are doing is greed. Greed will destroy our community more quickly than any cancer known.

In this valley bottom, our resources are limited and we must learn to maximize them. We need certain community installations that will take land. For the most part, these will not affect the arable, farmable land available to us as they will be either back up the dry draws or against the steeper ground. We will, therefore, have to limit the acreage available to each family in the valley. There is also, for us, unlimited acreage at the top of the grade that will be available to anyone who wants it."

"If this ash ever stops falling, there would well be a return to the dry land wheat farming that was so profitable before disaster struck. Again, that is for the future. We have no plans for that ground at this point. What we do have plans for is this valley."

"The area of Tumalum Creek will not be open for settlement as there is a very special species already living there that needs our help to survive. We have moved two couples into that area to act as curators for this sapient species... please notice I did not say sentient, for they are far beyond the merely sapient. They are reasoning, thinking, articulate beings that are very close to us in most ways. " With this, Jared stopped his discourse to allow his bombshell to sink in for a bit... and sink in it did... the meeting erupted!

With the expertise gained from long years spent addressing the public, Jared allowed the tumult to run its natural course as shouts for more information were heard and calls for specifics became more adamant. As in most such situations, the shock subsided and began to ebb while the mood shifted to a more "interested" mode. Eventually, calm returned and a spokesman had stepped forth from the group to ask for the attention of the Executive Committee. Again, Jared signaled to the waiting spokesman to be patient as he rapped his makeshift gavel sharply on his makeshift bench and asked for quiet to return.

"Now," the Chairman began, "thank you for your attention," he said to the gathered in general, Turning and addressing the waiting petitioner directly, he said, "Mr. Williams, do you have something for us?"

"It's Bill," he said firmly, "and I do have a question of general interest here... you have pretty much dropped a bombshell on us here and I'm sure we're all as curious as I am, but exactly what is this new species in our area? Is it something we should consider dangerous? Are we at risk from this species?"

Before an answer could be forthcoming, a feminine cry rang out from the assembly, "I knew we were selling our souls to the Devil for leaving town and coming to this God-forsaken place! We are all going to die in this wilderness and no one will ever know!"

Jared waited a moment longer to allow the hum to subside then began, "You are free to return to town at any time, ma'am... we do not intend to hold anyone here if they have no wish to be here. In fact, I suggest we give it a few days and see how many of you wish to return. If necessary, we can provide an escort for you as far as the flats and you can then proceed on your own. That, however, is for another time. What we have come here to discuss this evening is immediate."

"We have discovered proof of a species long postulated to exist but never definitively proven..."

"Are you talking about Bigfoot?" a cry rang from the assembly. "Please don't tell me you're going to try to perpetuate that myth again..."

"I am indeed talking about the species we called Sasquatch or Bigfoot before. And, before you start arguing the fact, we have a living, breathing clan residing in the canyons around the Anderssen place on Tumalum Creek just a few miles to the south of us..."

"My Gawd," a call came ringing out, "we need to exterminate them before they kill us all for our food!"

"Stop that kind of talk right now," Jared stated firmly. "There will be no genocide in our area at all. These are a living, viable group of people very near like us. They live well in their realm and, like us, they are devastated by this disaster. The local clan was surviving by utilizing the animals the Anderrsen's left behind. To that end, we have established a safe area for them there. Right now, we have four people earmarked as curators for their people and we will probably need a few more as time progresses."

As questions were shouted out, the man tried his best to answer them as others rose to help him from time to time. The discussion endured for nearly two hours when Jared raised his hand and called for quiet. "In time, we want everyone here to meet these beings, but we have to be very careful about that. They are like us in so many ways, but so unlike us in others. It is my understanding that there is nothing they do now that we, as a people could not once do. The fact is, however, we have left certain skills lapse as we developed."

"What kind of skills?" came from the group.

"For one thing, the ability to communicate non-verbally. I mean by direct thought transference."

When shouts of "I don't believe that..." and "That's pure hogwash" came from the crowd, Jared just raised his hands and said, "I am not here to argue the point, I am just passing on data from those working with that population. We will all find out for ourselves in short order, so let's leave this for that time, okay?"

Jared then turned the stage over to the chairman of the "Lands" Committee with the hope that this might get the new settler's minds off his news and on to the future again. As Art Linker rose, he asked his committee to come forth to help. As a unit, they unfolded a hand drawn map of the Tucannon River valley showing, roughly, the flow of the river, the side draws and the existing structures.

Art began by explaining that this map was only for reference for there would not be any claims allowed until the summer's work was done. "We will be very busy this summer," He began. "We have several indoor growing facilities that have been left to us and we intend to utilize them to the fullest

Valley of the Tucannon

extent, possible. Right here in the four building where we stand, we have over forty acres of potential cropland available to us on a year-round basis. We have removed the 'crop' that once grew there..." and as the laughter calmed, for no one had not heard what the original purpose of these sheds had been, he continued. "As was explained before we left the city, we have a plan that has been devised, discussed, defamed, diverted and delivered..." and he waited again for a moment to allow the enjoyment of his choice of words to wane.

"We have decided that we will be issuing 'work credit vouchers' for every hour spent in labor for the community this summer. Every person who works will receive these vouchers from the very young to the very old... from the unskilled to the engineer or doctor. There will be a division on credits earned made ONLY in view of the worker's age... and even there, the divisions are generous. Under six will receive one tenth credit per unit. Six through nine will receive one third credit per unit, ten through thirteen will receive one half credit per unit and fourteen through sixteen will receive eighty percent credit per unit. Anyone seventeen and older receives full credit per unit. There will be no division this year between one who weeds carrots and one who does brain surgery... if we have anyone who can do brain surgery. Is that clear?"

"When the time comes to select your property, for those who wish property of their own, we will have each plot measured and marked. There will be a limit of twenty acres for each adult couple or single adult. The Committee will handle the bidding. At no time will a single family unit control more than twenty acres of land."

"In the case of two land-holding single people becoming a couple in the eyes of the Committee, title to one or the other of the parcels will be remitted to the community. Our goal here, as agreed to by the body, is to ensure that every family has a plot of their own and that no family controls more than another family. In that view, no parcel will be allowed to be transferred to another entity. There will be no accumulations of land by an individual or a family. In all cases, here, the SPIRIT of the law will be enforced not the letter of the law. As we stated earlier, there are millions of acres of ground outside of this valley and we do not pretend to want to control that. We are only concerned with the arable ground along thirty miles of this river from where the old Camp was at the junction of this Tucannon Road and the road up Phillip's Grade and only from the river to the steep ground on each side, and to a lesser extent, the side valleys to the river itself... Are there any questions?"

When the tumult had subsided, Art handed the gavel over to the Chair of the Construction Committee who began softly. "My friends," Johnny Mancuso said in a soft but firm voice, "we need to outline our plan of action here. As you can imagine, the buildings you see here will be needed very soon for growing our winter's food. In the meantime, however, we will be using this first one as temporary quarters for most of you. I know we had hoped to be able to spread out more when we came from town, and we won't be nearly as crowded as we were in our potato shed apartments, but, for the time being we will be required to share accommodations. The shelters the advance crew built for us in advance of our arrival are nearly complete and we will be moving to those as they become available. Our goal is to have this facility free within a month."

"We have much to accomplish this summer. Our very survival depends on us growing enough food for our community and that will be done like the old Kibbutz system in Israel in the late forties and fifties... what is grown will be stored and used by the community as a whole. For the short term, we'll be sharing community meals and we will keep the team format system we've been using with twelve to fifteen people per mess. As we move to our own dwellings, this will, of course, decrease in scope and stature."

"Our first order of business will be to complete construction of the temporary housing begun by the advance team. We have a sign up roster here for the various jobs that will need doing. Those that have special skills will be given preference in assignment, but not in credit chits as was explained earlier. In our colony, for now, we will all earn the same per hour. Until this blessed ash stops falling, and that could be twenty years from now, we will need to keep our food production communal and our labor determined by our needs."

When the meeting was dismissed, there was a great deal of discussion of the basic facts presented with some of the people seeming to have heard all of this for the very first time. Some even talked about breaking away from this group and going it on their own, if not here, then in another valley nearby. The few hotheads fomenting this revolt were quickly singled out by Colonel Andy's peace keepers and brought into an audience with the colony leaders. It was explained to this group that they were under no duress to stay here and if they felt they'd be better served to be on their own, they were certainly welcome to move out at first light.

Colonel Andy, himself, explained that he could and would see them escorted back as far as the Dayton town site and they could determine their future from there. As there was an extreme shortage of working stock, none could be released to them, but the colony would allow their use as far as Dayton.

When they began to bluster that they had their rights, the colonel stopped them immediately and told them that, "Yes, you do have your rights. I have just explained them to you. You have the right to leave at any time. You do NOT have the right to create unrest of dissent in this colony. If you do that, you come under my auspices and I, should that happen, will simply carry you out of the canyon and turn you loose. If you decide to return, you will be shot on sight. Is that understood? Do I need to make it any clearer?" He then paused while one might count to ten slowly and said, simply, "I suppose that covers that, then?"

When he received an affirmative reply from each of these people, he said, quietly, "Dinner should be ready now. Get yourself some chow and a night's sleep for tomorrow brings a new era in our life."

Chapter 14
New Genesis

It was summer on the calendar, but one would never know it by looking at the world. Still, that terrible ash fell from a sodden, angry sky and covered everything it touched. Remarkably, spirits were high among the band of settlers who populated the valley now christened "New Genesis" for it was a new beginning. Although it had only 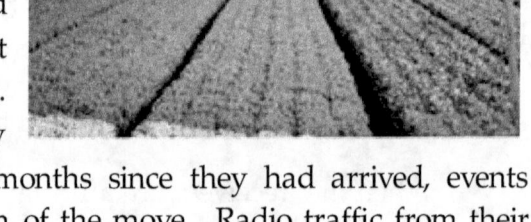 been less than three months since they had arrived, events had shown the wisdom of the move. Radio traffic from their former home in the city had diminished. Whether that was due to lack of power for the radios that talked to them or attrition was taking those who remained was not known.

Here in the valley, conditions were good. The settlers had finished all the housing needed for the entire colony and the covered growhouses were proving their worth with the bounty being brought forth from them. The original plan for a harvest of:

Dry Corn	20	ton
Carrots	4	ton
Spuds	16	ton
Turnips	4	ton
Beets	2	ton
Kohlrabi	2	ton

Cabbages	2	ton
Beans (aggregate)	16	ton
Squash (varieties)	10	ton

had been expanded now to include continuous plantings of

GreenBeans
Cauliflower
Broccoli
Okra
Lettuces
Cabbage
Corn

...since the houses were designed to grow crops year-round. There were even plantings of various melons and cucumbers to satisfy people's sweet tooth cravings. As people thought of other things they liked, and seeds were found, the plantings were expanded. Sugar beets were another staple that would be beneficial to the colony, but right now, they were not essential as honey form the colony's bees was providing the sugar necessary.

As soon as the various seeds were in the ground, the labor requirements for the farm nose-dived and a boon was found when it was realized that children and young adults would be well suited to tending the growth beds. The youngsters were concerned how they were going to get hours in to earn their own credits and this served that need well. Of course their school was still their main job and willing teachers came forth to make sure this need was met.

With the necessities of food being attended to, the colony turned to the next items on their growing list... capital improvements.

Two things the colony knew they would need soonest were some form of electrical power generation capability and a mill for grinding grains and a sawmill for making dimension lumber. There were people within the colony more than willing to step up to undertake the task that ranged from laborers to engineers. In the end, the committee recommended they go with their original suggestions and have the engineer, Cynthia Pryor, head a group of people qualified to perform the needed tasks to make the wind generator they had scavenged from the wind farm at the top of the grade operate with water power as their energy source.

It was decided that to rely on wind in this remote spot would not be wise as they did not have access to a constant supply of batteries to supplant the lack of energy when the wind was not blowing. Water, while it did have certain drawbacks like its tendency to freeze in low temperatures, was, at least constant in flow if the temperatures stayed above fourteen degrees Fahrenheit.

Also, with this constant ash fall, the temperatures did not get so extremely cold... it was like it served as an atmospheric insulator. Further, to prevent the flume that was projected

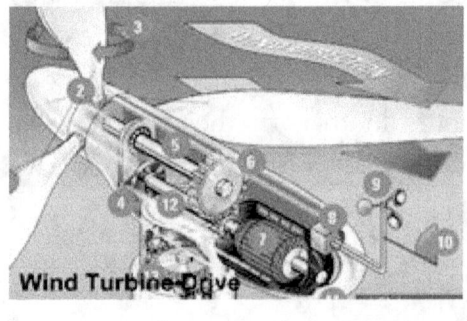

Wind Turbine Drive

to be built to provide the water to power the generator from becoming a sort of giant sluice box for the heavy ash falling that it would be covered. The ash that covered it would then provide a degree of insulation within the flume to protect the water to an even lower temperature. At this point, no one knew what that number would be, but even a couple of degrees would be significant.

The engineering for the actual generator was really quite simple. The system was designed for the windmill to turn at twenty seven revolutions per minute (rpm). The team had already devised and were using a scheme that converted the

Covered Flume

fifteen rpm they could get on their water wheel to nearly eight hundred rpm to turn the automotive alternators they used for lighting areas within homes, barracks and, most especially, the infirmary. With that knowledge in hand, it took little more ingenuity to gear their wheel to get the optimum twenty seven rpm the big turbines needed... a simple two to one step down was all that was needed.

While the engineering crew constructed the parts necessary to make the unit operate efficiently in the application they had planned, the dirt movers went to work to construct a ditch and flume to provide the energy necessary to turn the wheels that would turn the gear that would turn the smaller gear that would...

It was decided to utilize the flow from a healthy spring that lay back up one of the draws off the main valley. Some hard work and clever digging created a constant water flow that was deemed more than sufficient for the task at hand. One major serendipity of using the energy of flowing water is that its force is not diminished by a single use. No water is removed from the system and it continues to flow on down the flume, always storing more energy in that flow. As long as gravity was available to replenish the energy lost turning one wheel, it would turn another... then another. On this one waterway, the team ultimately installed five of the commandeered wind turbines.

When the water had passed the last of the five turbines, it was not done yet. Down the canyon just a bit the construction crews were busy answering a huge need in the new community. With so many people now coming into this valley to live, a constant and liquid supply of dimension lumber was rapidly becoming a necessity and by winter that need was projected to become dire. By then, people would have chosen their stake acreage and would be thinking about their own homes and outbuildings. For the time being, it was just a dream as the ever falling ash was so heavy on a standard roof, that they simply could not survive. Everywhere, there were buildings disappearing beneath the ash and being crushed to nothingness by the weight.

The Committee had long discussions addressing the question of whether to combine the grist mill with the sawmill and drive them both by the same wheel. The arguments centered around the time and effort required to construct a second wheel and building balanced against the problems of the grain mill and the sawmill coexisting in a single setting. After much disagreement and conjecture, it was suggested that ideas be polled from the community concerning this. Required contingent with the idea was the need for a workable schematic for implementing said plans. It was hoped this would limit the input of fanciful ideas and thoughts... a wish that was only partly fulfilled, however.

When a workable plan was devised that housed the grist mill in the upper half of a two level structure with the sawmill downstairs, the committee adopted this strategy. The plan called for the mill wheel to turn a geared hub that would, in turn, power a vertical shaft. It was this vertical shaft that would run from upstairs where it powered the mill stones to  the lower level where it powered two vertical sash saws.

The water coming off the wheel was not done yet. Although the crew had used all the energy they could get from the falling water, it still had a major purpose left... from the mill, it held in a large pond below the wheel awaiting the day when an intricate system of irrigation canals would wend their way downstream to provide the liquid life needed to produce crops in this desert land. The ditches and those farms were in the future, however as the ash continued to fall, though not as heavy in this protected valley as in the open lands outside of the valley. It would do no good to dig ditches and pipe water in systems that would soon clog themselves with tons of ash. It was as well to wait until the ash decided to stop before construction would begin on these huge projects. That did not stop the planners from doing

Simple Double Sash Mill

the surveying necessary to determine the feasibility of the project and allow those concerned to estimate the resources necessary for it.

Cal Greenwood was a robust man of just more than fifty years of age who had not really suffered from illness throughout his life. He was enjoying his part in the building of the road that would bring the logs from the area above the old camp at Wooten to the mill being finished now down the river a ways. For the most part they had simply cleared and used the old Tucannon River Road that had wound its way up the scenic valley before this disaster had

Forwarding the Logs

begin, but there were areas where the work was arduous to make the way passable for the log wagons the colony had built for this purpose.

It was midafternoon when Cal started feeling dizzy and a bit faint... he knew not why, but he stopped and found a place amid the falling powder to sit and let this pass. He had skipped his lunch today because they were on a particularly critical area that needed to be completed quickly. Besides, he reasoned, he could use the extra work credits the overtime would give him. He had found a particularly pretty little piece of land that would suit him very well and, while it was still a few months before anyone could officially bid on properties, he knew if he had the most credit, he'd stand in good stead to get his choice. The man was thinking just of this when his head started to swim and he suddenly just crumpled to the ground.

Larry Singleton was his work partner and it was he who saw Cal fall. Immediately, he sang out for some help and ran to his partner's side. Larry saw immediately that Cal was not getting enough air... his lips were blue and he started at once to administer cardio pulmonary resuscitation to his friend and called once more for help. In moments, a small group had gathered around Cal and orders were given for the wagon to be brought round so they could get him to the infirmary as quickly as possible.

As quickly as the rescue crew had loaded Cal into the wagon bed with Larry staying right with him to continue the CPR that all had learned only recently at a safety meeting, they departed downstream to the little infirmary in hopes they could get help there.

The trip seemed to take hours and hours to the anxious men who were designated to accompany the stricken man to his aid. In fact it took less than one half hour to make the trek in the horse drawn wagon, one of many now at work in the valley.

As the team pulled up to the gate, the on duty medical staff moved Cal quickly inside where the best doctor they had available for this kind of problem, Dr. Kyle Stacy, went to work on him. In the time since the destruction had struck, many useful tools and devices had been manufactured by the clever colonists and the medical staff had not lacked in this either. Although his tools were crude when compared to those he had before the disaster, this doctor was by no means without help. He had a respirator of sorts that had been devised. It was simple, but it was effective and even was powered electrically since this area was the first to receive power from the generating devices.

By the time Dr. Kyle, as everyone called him, had completed his examination, he knew the man had suffered a myocardial infarction... a heart attack... and he did not hold out much hope for the man. While there were many things they were equipped to handle here, something as serious as this was not part of that. He was seriously afraid that this man was doomed. He simply had no equipment to deal with this kind of condition and surgery of this magnitude was out of the question... he simply did not have the means for it.

While the doctor worked his best magic, even with is resuscitator, working smoothly, the messenger was dispatched to locate Cal's wife Emma and to return her here to be with him. Amazingly, Cal held his own and his body continued to function, albeit weakly, in his greatly diminished condition.

As soon as Emma arrived, she was apprised of the situation and told of the prognosis. She insisted her husband would survive this against all odds and the doctor just smiled at her and shook his head in agreement while withholding his own opinion as he knew it would do no good to render it.

Chapter 15
New Medicines

A few miles up the road from the infirmary on the Andersson place, recently rechristened "Sasquatch Ranch", a cry rang out to the caretakers there. Quickly, Jenna responded to the summons issued by Kenora.

"What is it? Why are you upset?" she asked the large being who was literally shaking as he stood before her. It was unusual enough for the big fellow to show himself though the young ones were often seen on the hills near the center of the ranch.

"There is tragedy in the place of the doctors of your people. You are needed there immediately, my young woman," stated the largest of the clan who lived here. *"Please take yourself there at once."*

Jenna called to her mates here and told them what she had just learned and, turning back to Kenora, she said, "Kenora, I'm not sure I'm knowledgeable enough to help. You have been teaching me much about the medicinal arts of herbs, but I'm very afraid." Even as she spoke, she could see a vision in her mind of what was happening at the infirmary. She saw the man on the bed... the nurses assisting a doctor who she knew at once was Dr. Kyle...

"Do not be of fear, little one," he stated firmly. *"We would not have chosen you if we had not confidence in you. I will be with you, in your mind as I am here and I will*

guide you to do the things you will need to know. Go you now, Jenna, and do that which is necessary."

As the young woman turned to ask of her mates what she should do, no words were necessary for there was her husband, Bud, with her favorite little pinto mare saddled and as he held out the reins, she simply folded into his arms and quivered there a moment. She could feel the power of the Primal Man who had tagged her for this task as she thanked her man for being so considerate of her. As she opened her mouth to thank him, he just kissed her lightly and said, "Go, darling girl... we will be along as soon as we finish feeding. We're nearly done now, so we won't be far behind you. You are needed there and that is your place for now. Hurry now and get along. We have everything well under control here and we're so proud that you are being called for this."

Quickly she glanced at Kayla and Eric who both nodded at her in confirmation of all that Bud had said. With nothing more to add, she simply nodded, turned, mounted her horse and started down the mountain at a comfortable canter.

"Do not stay here to feed the animals," the large fellow said. *I will have Inisha and Aranya complete that for you. It is far more important that you be with Jenna now. Take your horses and go quickly. It is important that she took these first steps on her own but now she will need your support... give it freely."*

Doctor Kyle was less than ecstatic to see Jenna come charging into his clinic while raving about helping his patient. He felt there was no way this youngster could have any knowledge that would help Cal in his desperate situation. It was his nurses on duty that finally calmed the distressed doctor.

The girl had just been admitted to the small enclave set aside as a resting room for the stricken man when a buzzing sound began to be heard. She was confused by what she was hearing, but she knew better than to question its source as she watched the man's chest begin to vibrate. On and on the hum continued and even grew in volume.

Dr. Kyle seemed a bit distressed by what was happening in his clinic, but, truth told, he knew of nothing more that was available to him and he'd seen too many miracles in his life with people he knew had lived their lives out who suddenly recovered from seemingly fatal diseases to continue being contributing members of the society. With this in mind, he was willing to watch what happened... to an extent...

As the persistent buzz deepened in intensity, Jenna motioned to Dr. Kyle to approach more closely, then asked him to perform whatever he did to monitor the man's blood pressure and pulse rate. As soon as the doctor placed his stethoscope on the man's chest, he could tell there was improvement in his heart's work... it no longer sounded so labored and he quickly asked Janine to do a blood pressure reading.

The hum settled into a quiet buzz and continued while the girl held his left arm and stroked him softly on the upper abdomen. She turned to the doctor and asked, "Do you have any extract of that large, pretty plant that grows in the spring and has a line of flower all up the stem? The flowers bloom in succession beginning at the bottom and moving to the top."

It was one of the nurses who recognized her description and turned to the doctor and said, "I believe she means Foxglove, Doctor. I think she's asking for that."

"Yes," Jenna answered quickly, "The leaves are good for the heart."

An amazed Dr. Kyle looked at her and said, "How do you understand the use of Digitalis for treating heart ailments? I've used it for years, and knew it was made from that plant, but I have no idea how to do so."

Just take the leaves, dried if we have them and make a tea from it. He will be able to take tea soon. This thing the Sasquatch People are doing here will help him tremendously."

The girl had no more than finished that statement than Cal's eyes opened tentatively... like a man waking to a bright light in his eyes. Slowly he became more sure of himself and looked around quickly as if to locate himself in his confusion. He had, after all, passed out while out in the open and was now in a bed inside a closed building. He soon saw his wife and the corner of his mouth tried to turn up into a smile... an effort that was just too much for him as of yet.

Janine stepped in quickly to stop the man from moving around and told him to just relax. "You've been through an ordeal, Cal, so don't strain now. This young woman and her 'friends' helped you through a tough time but I think the worst has passed now. We will need to monitor you very closely for a bit, but I think the crisis has passed now too."

As soon as the nurse spoke, Cal calmed and smiled a small, resigned smile and lay back calmly. He sighed a welcome, "Thank you!" to the lady and visibly relaxed, looking to his rather pretty, if harried wife at his side.

It was dark outside when things around the clinic calmed sufficiently for Dr. Kyle to call Jenna into his cubicle of an office... He began, "Young lady, that was probably the most vehement and profound demonstration of 'Natural Medicine' I have ever seen. What you did and the results were absolutely spectacular! Just how old are you and where did you learn such a wonderful procedure and, even more importantly, can you teach me?"

"Doctor," the young girl began, "I am just seventeen years old, but I have been studying with an ancient people for whom this is their only way of medicine. They are masters at natural healing and the use of herbs..."

"But, what was that buzzing sound... that vibration I saw and felt..." the doctor interrupted... "I've never seen anything like that! It was absolutely astounding how the man responded!"

"That was a procedure that my Teachers did, Doctor. I had nothing to do with that exercise," the girl explained. "They did tell me that it was a treatment for the heart."

"It was that!" Doctor Kyle exclaimed... "It is now as though he has never suffered that attack as far as his heart is concerned. I don't know what they did or how they did it, but I would certainly love to be able to do it. Do you think they would teach me?"

For just a moment, Jenna's focus was lost as she concentrated on the message coming to her directly from her Teacher... slowly she returned to her own bright self and replied, "No, Doctor, that will not be possible. It is something they must do... it is an ancient method of energy manipulation that we as humans have lost the ability to control. Perhaps in the future it will be possible to train a human in the way of the forces, but it is not so today. In the meantime, please know that they will be available through me to you for whatever you need."

"That's disappointing," the doctor confessed, "but I understand what he means. I have never seen anything so profound as what I witnessed today... do you think it would be possible for me to attend your Teacher and learn somethings I need to know for what we face now?"

Jenna quietly stated, "Come to the Ranch when you can get away and we will do what we can. We understand your need for remedial teachings as conditions have now changed. Come as soon as you can without jeopardizing this man."

Both Jenna and the doctor knew this interview was at an end, so stood and after exchanging pleasantries and mutual thanks, they separated. Doctor Kyle to his home and his wife and Jenna to find her mate and her cohorts.

Chapter 16
A New Society

There was no break in the steadily falling ash as there had been none for all these years. Kayla stood by the fireplace in the living room of her Sasquatch Ranch headquarters and looked at those gathered. It was a young group, as was their colony in general. Few oldsters survived the initial disaster  and of those that did, many succumbed to the conditions that followed. The hard life in the city took its toll and two epidemics here in their valley home had been hard on both the very old and the very young.

Two years had passed since an outbreak of Legionairre's Disease had taken a toll on the older element in the colony's population. The outbreak had been caused by a water system contaminated by the falling ash. That system fed the building housing the oldest of the residents, probably the worst possible place to strike. Eleven people died before the pneumonia-like disease was identified and its cause isolated. Fortunately, this is not a disease that is transmitted from person to person so isolation was not necessary and the outbreak was stemmed. Repairing the affected water system was not so easy, however and the panic it caused in other domicile barns was not easy to overcome as well. Eventually, however, things returned to normal after all the various water systems were tested and found to be free of the bacterium that caused the outbreak.

An influenza outbreak the following winter was also hard on the very young. Conditions reminiscent of those in 1918 led to the same net result with the loss of some of the youngest in the colony. Deaths were held to but three, but that was three too many in a colony closely connected as this one.

Communications between the sasquatch people and the humans had increased with major kudos being heaped on the ancient ones for their help in effecting a cure for most disease outbreaks. Losses in their ranks had been low but significant with the death of one of the patriarchs of the local clan.

That, in fact, was the reason for this gathering today. The human element was taking advantage of the invitation to the old fellow's, Gornoah, by name, funeral. Death among the sasquatch people had been so rare that most humans did not even know they conducted rituals or burials for death. The two couples charged with taking care of this ranch and managing the affairs of the sasquatch people had been most surprised by the invitations they had received for anyone interested to attend the ritual for the passing of old Gornoah. They knew that these people conducted these rituals but even they did not know of what they consisted.

The sun had yet to make its appearance this morning as some two dozen humans and fifteen sasquatch people made their way to the upper end of Tumalum Creek to an area where some pines still grew among the outcroppings of granite found there. It was on a north facing slope that the group was brought to a halt at the top of a low ridge that divided this creek's drainage from Cummings Creek just to the west. On a promontory of that ridge, resplendent with a crown of Ponderosa Pine that was still, after over eight years of constant ashfall, green and vibrant, if not as growing and alive as it had been prior to the advent of the fall. A large, almost silver colored female stepped to the front of the group of sasquatch gathered there and began speaking aloud.

Some would have called it a chatter, had they heard it, and certainly, no human here could understand her words, but the intent was obvious... she was telling the gathered about the life of this venerated male who had passed from this life to the next. Dr. Kyle, one of those invited who had no plans to NOT be there listened intently to the dissertation and, although he didn't understand the words, loved hearing them. He was so deeply intent here, that he literally jumped when a voice spoke into his mind...

"Would you like to 'hear' her words so you might understand?" the voice intoned directly into his mind.

"I most surely would, if that would be allowable," he responded almost too rapidly.

At once, he understood, in his mind, the words he was hearing from this large, silver lady! He was fascinated in her discourse and was almost too fixated to listen to the content as thrilled as he was with the fact that he COULD hear. Quickly, however, he recovered and paid close

216

attention as she delivered probably the most eloquent example of the rendering of a man's life he had ever heard.

She told of his genealogy for many generations, and, while it meant nothing to him directly, he could tell by the nodding heads of the other large beings in attendance that this was not true of them. They not only understood the words of this wonderful eulogy, they knew the people mentioned. It seemed that many of them might be recalled in their own genealogies when their time on earth was done.

While the dissertation seemed but a couple of minutes, the clock told the people differently when she finished. It seems she had spoken for nearly three hours while the invited guests listened patiently and totally enthralled by that which they were hearing.

On that lonely ridge top in a land of ash and gray, the next speaker, a younger male, took up the liturgy with a catalog of his progeny. This young man, and Kyle had the distinct impression he was a son or grandson of the old man told of all who owed their very existence to this male. He spoke of the mate of Gornoah, Argalah, who, it turns out, had been the first speaker, and of their five generations now living on earth. He spoke of the feats and capabilities of these generations of offspring who had contributed so much to the well-being of the people in general.

"Gornoah was not been born in this land," the younger man stated. *"He came here from those hot, steamy lands far to the southeast where he was reared in the swamps away from the humans. In those days,"* he stated, *"there was not good feelings shared with the hairless ones. There were many there who considered out people to be*

217

monsters and wanted to kill us off. It was the work of many generations to cause this terrible condition to go away and control people no more."

"Unfortunately, it was this terrible falling ash that ended that period. Where Gornoah lived as a young man, he was often hunted. Of course he thought this funny and he easily evaded those inept beings with their ineffective guns. He often teased them by sneaking in close to them and making an utterance that they thought meant they were about to be eaten! He would then sneak away to hide while these young men ran through the swamps with their noisy craft that propelled them on the water with wind."

In the ways of our people, when he became of age to be considered mateable, his name was put forth at the Clan Gathering in in the far north by the lake called Louise. It was the spring of Argalah who had just reached eighteen years and was, herself, of an age to take a mate. She heard of this brave and accomplished man who lived in the great swamp by the southern gulf and was intrigued by him. She stated that she had interest and would travel to his clan to see if this might not come to pass."

The young man continued telling how the woman, in the manner of the Hairy People, traveled to his clan and spent the summer becoming acquainted with the handsome man. "She really did not need the summer. She has told me many times how she knew immediately that he was to be her mate, but she didn't want him to know how taken she was with him or he'd be insufferable."

When the union was agreed upon, the newly mated couple returned to the clan of her people to live, for does not a woman need her mother in times of stress and of child birth? *"This is why our people do it this way,"* he stated to the hairless ones present, for why would he say something like that to his own people who already knew that.

He further explained that it was necessary to travel such long distances to take a mate because their population was never high and they knew the dangers of having children with someone who is too closely related to you. This caused Dr. Kyle to shake his head slowly while thinking that this made imminent good sense.

When finished, the clan prepared the grave site for the esteemed Gornoah. A rocky promontory was prepared and a deep hole dug wherein the body of the great being was placed. When he was in the grave, he was covered with the hides of elk and some few personal items were placed into the grave with him. There were not many items as this is not an acquisitive species, and many of the items were curious, to say the least. There were no tools as you would expect to see in the graves of the ancient peoples of this continent. There were no weapons. There were a very few rocks that had either interesting shapes or were broken into interesting forms. Some showed a face, others just special colors. One thing placed with him by his mate was a tiny metal toy car that had come to him, no one knew how... but he had it and he had revered it all his life, so it was tendered to him for his journey into the next life.

The next step was to cover the body of the deceased and this was accomplished not with mere soil, but with with the great granite stones that had been removed in the excavation of the grave. When completed, a large pine tree was planted over the grave itself to disguise its purpose and to deny that any grave even existed at this place. When this  tree was in place, copious amounts of pine needles were strewn about made to look like they had naturally fallen from the recently transplanted tree. The overall effect, when complete was to deny that any grave had ever existed here. To anyone coming on this scene, it would appear solely that a pine tree was making a meager living from a rather inhospitable ridge top under difficult conditions.

Suddenly, there was a tension in the air... a soft, gentle breeze touched a sound that was even softer and it took the hairless ones a few moments to realize this was a form of chant arising from the throats of their hosts. More than a few of those assembled with the ancient race felt an urge to join in this call... most seemed to realize it was a final saying of goodbye to an old and dear friend... one who they would not see again in this life, but who was, obviously, not departed forever. Like the ship that departs the shore of this land those ashore say "Lo, she goes..." while those on the far shore say, "Lo, she comes"... so it is with those who depart us in this life... it is but temporary... but profound...

The mood on the return was somber, but not oppressive. It was quiet, but not silent. People talked about what they had witnessed and the large, hairy ones walked beside the hairless ones although to do so meant they had to slow their pace considerably. The feeling of love that prevailed was what the Prime Creator had meant in the beginning but had taken this many millennia and a disaster to accomplish, it would seem.

Slowly the entourage flowed back down the mountainside to the ranch itself. Most of the sasquatch people didn't stay, but returned to their duties, but the hairless ones, almost as one, filed into the ranch house and found a seat

Food and drink was offered and many partook, but some did not. People were quiet for the most part, thinking of what they had just witnessed and in which they had participation. The effects were deep. For so many lifetimes, those who spoke of this people were castigated, ridiculed and denigrated for their simple belief. So many had made contact but had denied it simply because they could not stand their family acting as they did. Too many demanded proof simply as a way to vindicate themselves and their actions, not to help these people any. Hence it was not forthcoming. Now, no one could deny... at least, no one in this region!

When most people had enjoyed a repast and refreshed with a drink, Jenna stood and began. "People, we need to move along here. The day is waning and we have much to discuss. I do want you to know there are beds and accommodations for all who wish to stay over since I know we will be going late into the night." The woman addressed a sizable crowd as many more had arrived since the group attending the funeral had departed. This meeting was scheduled to begin at three pm and it was now just minutes past that.

She began, "Let's begin with the annual report of the Committee of the Whole on the status of the colony and all that pertains to it." With that, Jenna called Adam Stuart to the front and handed him the gavel that signified that he held the staff and the meeting was his to continue from this point forward.

"First," the chairman began, "we have a report from 'town'... it seems there is no longer a town to be considered. As you know, we sent a squad into the old Tri-Cities area to investigate. They found nothing save a few old, caved in buildings. There was no sign of any living being there. No people appeared to exist at this time. They were diligent in investigating those areas that held remnant populations when last we knew and there is nothing there. There is not a sign of any life in that entire area..."

"The marauding gangs that were in evidence on our last investigation are no longer there. It is impossible to tell if they left or succumbed to conditions, but the fact is, they are no more in that area. There has been no abatement of ashfall in that area in eight full years now... it is not even partially protected as we are here in our enclave but receives the full brunt of the fall. The squad leader's report reads like

222

he was observing the Sahara Desert as far as life is concerned."

"With this being the case, the squad took extreme caution in exploring other places that had held people and found none anywhere... Bart Roberts had reported that his radio contacts were gone. He'd had several in the urban areas around Seattle, but they'd, one by one gone offline. Most had done so because they were out of food and had to try to locate some. The omnipresent roving gangs were disappearing rapidly and, other than a small colony here and there they could still raise, it appeared that the entire Pacific Northwest had been depeopled. There had to be small remnant pockets like our own from place to place, but there were not many. So much luck had gone into our saving that it simply could not have repeated that often."

"In short," the man continued, "until further data makes itself known, we should consider ourselves to be the last remnant of humanity left of earth and proceed as if that is the case."

A hubbub arose with that statement as people refused to believe that possible and really did not wish it to be the case.

"No!" screamed out several people at once, "We cannot be all there is... there must be more somewhere."

A small, slender, rather pretty woman stood up and asked permission to speak. At a nod from Jared she continued, "There simply has to be more people than this tiny group left living. I know it's been eight years now, but there were over six billion people on the earth when this happened, there just cannot be only a few hundred left and all in this one lone place. I agree we had great good fortune to have some people escape the initial disaster and your church, Jared, was very instrumental in saving so many with their doctrine... but we can't be all there is... What about Utah? That was full of people like you... would not some of those have survived?"

"Actually," Jared started, "I quite feel they could have... but we have no contact with them, nor has there been any radio contact with them in all this time. My heart tells me yes, but even if they are there, they may as well be on the dark side of the moon at this point."

"I take your point," the girl who called herself Ariana stated. "There may be a million people there, but they are as lost to us as if they were on Hawaii and the bridge is down!"

A smattering if laughter eased the tension of this line of thought somewhat and Jared continued, "I understand there may well be some viable populations here and there... I sure hope and pray there are, at least. But, they don't have any effect on us be they there or not. We are here and we are all we have. It COULD well be that if we don't survive, the human race will disappear from the universe. It COULD be that we are the last bastion of humanity in that universe. If this is true, we need to act like it. We have been fighting a holding action here, but we are not winning. We have had deaths and, overall, our population has decreased. We cannot sustain ourselves unless this trend is reversed. We need a baby boom..."

In the uproar that followed this statement, Jared just stood and listened while people vented their steam over this thought. While one could have counted to a hundred, there was little more than bedlam and turmoil but eventually, one voice found its way to the fore... "How are we ever going to support more people if this ash keeps falling?"

"Good point, Wade," answered Jared quietly, "but if we allow our population to die off below sustainable levels, it will make no difference whether the ash falls or not, mankind will simply disappear. It is the contention of our large, hairy friend, Kenorah, that the  ashfall is diminishing and will stop soon..."

Again, the volume went up with disparaging remarks predominating. Statements like "How the hell would they know?" and "That's BS..." led the way but Jared let the protests run their course before answering...

"You have no idea how disappointed I am to hear the responses we have just heard. After all how many of us have friends or family that have been saved by these people? Their medical skills are outstanding and they have been teaching herbal cures to all who would listen. We have found them to be universally helpful and intelligent beyond belief. To have them denigrated like some 1950s racial slur is beyond my ability to understand. I think it's probably time for me to resign this position now and return to my

225

own family. We have our stake acres now... all of us have and we're just waiting to be able to start making them productive anyway."

Over the objections of the vast majority of those assembled, Jared was adamant and tendered his resignation effective as soon as his replacement can be located and installed. It was time for the young family man to leave his public office and return to his own interests and goals.

Jenna stood and took the gavel back from the man as he returned to his seat. She looked over the still protesting group and said, "I think, in view of what has happened here, we should adjourn this meeting at this point and let the committee decide their course at which time another gathering will be called and whatever ratification that is needed will be called for. Do I have a motion and second on that?"

When it had been moved and seconded, the woman called for all in favor and then those opposed. Although there were substantially more nays than they were used to seeing, the motion was carried and the meeting adjourned for the time being.

Chapter 17
The End of the Fall

On the calendar, it said June Twenty-first but to the world of survivors it was unique and a day that would live forever in their memories... it was the day that the ash stopped falling. Eight and an half years it had been steady. There had been no break from its falling gray form since that terrible night a lifetime and a lifestyle away.

Gone were the comfortable homes in a medium to small city in a land based on freedom... though that had been ever eroding as well. Gone were the supermarkets and the Wal-Marts and the Sears stores... they simply had vanished overnight that December night so long ago. Life as had been known for generations was gone. As far as this colony knew, they were the only people living on earth. Out of Africa, though pretty thoroughly dismissed as a plausible theory before the fall of that heavenly body did not hold any interest or sway with this small group of survivors living in a snug valley in the far Pacific Northwest of the Nation that had once been known as America. Today it was merely known as "The River"... and it nurtured a band of strong and strong willed people.

There were fewer than five hundred souls here, up from the approximately two hundred fifty who began here those long years past. Most of the additions came about naturally, but there were a few who had straggled in from isolated pockets of survivors and made a place for themselves here. Subsequent expeditions to their places of origin added a few more to the Colony's number, but for the most part, seldom were found any survivors at the places from whence these stragglers had originated. Generally speaking, no one ever knew the fate of those who stayed behind to wait on rescue... other than to say rescue never came for them.

It was the first time, the inaugural day of a new train of thought for these survivors. They knew they would persevere in this life now. They knew that life would succeed... that children would be born and live a full life to die in their old age as it should be. They had beaten the worst that had been thrown at them... and they had Allies!

A species that had only been rumored of for so many generations before this disaster were now an integral part of this new society. The large, homanid peoples known simply as sasquatch people were now living alongside the human population. In fact, it had been the help received from this species in the form of natural medicine and healing that had saved the lives of many in the Colony, and, perhaps, even the Colony itself. Certainly, without their knowledge of the magic of the herbs growing, the people would have never known how to maintain themselves without the drugs of modern society.

With the ash not falling, the Committee, under its new chair, Will Baylor, recommended that as much exposed soil as could be covered be seeded with anything that would grow as soon as possible. It was greatly feared that enormous dust storms would be spawned by the summer winds blowing over this very fine, very loose ash that covered the country to an unestimated depth. With large quantities of wheat available, that quickly became the seed of choice though none knew the fate of the planting since it was well out of phase with the norm.

Although wheat in this country was normally planted in later summer and fall to yield a crop the following early summer, an actual crop was less the goal here as was ground stabilization. If the there was any wheat produced, and the committee felt the chance of that was small, it would simply be allowed to fall to the ground to reseed.

In the lower areas, along the river itself, large areas of alfalfa were seeded. It was hoped that is crop would take hold and do well. Being a perennial type of plant, high in protein, it was much desired. It was not expected that much in the way of actual benefit would be produced this year beyond that needed to feed the colony's rabbit population, but the basis would be established for the return of the husbandry of other species as well, both domestic and wild. It had been a major focus for the entire time of the ashfall to find hidden, surviving alfalfa stacks that could be used to sustain not only the colony's embryonic herd of stock such as the cattle, goats and a few llamas as well as various other species of ruminants, but the small numbers of elk, deer, turkeys and other, smaller species that were so  prevalent here prior to the disaster. It was felt that this may well be the only source for seed stock for these native species in all of North America. If that were so, this small population of animals may well have to serve to repopulate the entirety of their former range.

Certainly, in their travels, the colonists, well trained in searching out surviving species, had found no evidence of such. Admittedly, they had covered only a small portion of the entire of even what had been the eastern part of what had been the state of Washington, but it was an area that, prior to the devastation, supported very large populations of mule deer as well as the tiny whitetail found throughout eastern Washington and Idaho. It was common, while hunting in the "Time Before," as that era was becoming known, to see over three hundred deer a day, today, in the after, except near the designated feeding stations, none were seen. All hoped that this would change with a return to some degree of normalcy in the Time After.

With an eye to this replanting effort, it was proposed to the Committee that an expedition be mounted to some of the huge, towering grain storage silos that still stood out as a stark reminder of what had once been. Of course all the sheet metal covered structures were gone and buried under several feet of ash, but there were some of the concrete construction towers still intact. For the purposes of this effort, it would not matter if the grain had been contaminated with ash, only that it be viable seed. Even if the germination rate was very low, that would not matter as there was a huge supply available to anyone who could mine their way into these structures.

Of more immediate concern was finding stocks of alfalfa seed in the quantities needed... it was pointed out that the alfalfa could well be intermixed with pasture grasses for the colony's short term purposes. Since high grade dairy quality alfalfa was not needed, but a more general purpose cattle and horse feed, pure stands of alfalfa were not necessary.

Kenorah suggested that he send Inisha and Aranya with the party to help as they could. It was still expected that any expedition could find remnant populations at any time and, at this late stage, they would not be expected to be friendly or cooperative. Kenorah explained that, especially, Inisha had abilities to protect the teams that they may not have on their own.

The Committee called a team leader and briefed her as to the goals of the trip and asked for her best recommendations as to the make-up of the team. Sary McDowell Baylor accepted graciously and then proceeded to ask for experienced planters and residents of the local area to help. The woman's logic was simple but correct... the planters would know what they were needing and the local residents would know where it was located. She opted for twenty five people and ten wagons with stout teams to make the trek.

The first trek was planned to the Dayton townsite area as there were not only the grain grower's elevators there, but there was also a large farmer's coop store located in the former town. It was collapsed and buried to be sure, but its location was known and, since the town had died entirely in one night with no survivors ever found, there was a good chance that it had not been pilfered or looted since.

The sun was shining the morning the caravan had set for their target for the trek... the sun... it was difficult to imagine that these people would ever see it again after eight and a half years without having done so. It was glorious in its splendor hanging high in the eastern sky, peering down over the Clearwater Ridge into the valley of the Tucannon. There was not a person present who was not eternally grateful for its presence!

Quietly, the young woman and mother rode back along her line, checking with her team captains to ensure all was in readiness for this trip. As it turned out, in the end, she had four teams of eight persons each and each led by a Captain. In addition to this human contingent, there were two large, hairy and entirely competent members of the sasquatch community resident near the human colony. After ensuring that everything was as ready as human hands could make them, she raised her hand and let out the time honored call, "yoooooooo..." as her upraised hand dropped to point the way of the exodus up the grade from her home ranch and thence across the high prairie to Whetstone and then into the site of Dayton.

As one, the twelve wagons began to roll out. Slowly, the train started up the severe grade toward their goals. It was expected that the train would reach Dayton by midday and would begin immediately to gain entry to the stored grain they hoped to find in abundance in the old grain growers elevators there. They knew that the elevators would be inoperable, but they hoped to be able to devise a way of getting access and removing grain without the need for electrical power.

There had been several ideas advanced for doing this and the committee designed to find a way had found merit in a several schemes. In their efforts, they had called in the authors of those schemes to explain them in great detail to the committee. They then choose three such and asked the person proposing the idea to accompany the team on their trek. All were most willing and instantly included!

As the cavalcade creeped up the steep grade, the two special guests, Inisha and Aranya walked at the head of the column. Very few rode on this steep grade as the stock needed every advantage to climb out and certainly the extreme weight of the two moving on their own was appreciated by the stock pulling the freight wagons!

Only a few of the trekkers knew they were in the vicinity of one of the current feeding stations for a sizeable band of mule deer and elk. It was the two sasquatch people who recognized the situation first and they both stopped immediately and watched the herd standing in the distance. Inisha stopped the procession and said, *"Let's not disturb those animals..."*

Sary looked at him and asked, "How can we not disturb them, we have to pass very near them as we round this next curve?"

A deep chuckle rumbled from deep in the young man's huge chest as he said, merely, *"Watch!"*

Suddenly it was like there was a shimmer in the air and the deer began looking around like what they had been watching had disappeared. They appeared nervous at first, but it only took moments for the herd to calm and return to eating and doing the things deer do when finishing breakfast and preparing to a day in their bed. It was obvious that they simply did not see the caravan as it made its way past them and on around the next curve in the road. There were more than a few who were curious as to what had happened. Only a few knew that the sas people had done something to make it happen, but all knew that it was not a normal occurrence.

When the entire entourage had cleared the area and would not further disturb the animals, Sary approached the large pair and said, "Okay, my friends, what just happened here? What did you do?"

Again that deep, rumbling chuckle came floating up... *"I cloaked us,"* Inisha stated in a very matter of fact way.

Sary and those who were close enough to have heard that went totally quiet. After one could have counted to twenty five slowly, she asked, "How did you do that? At no time could I not see those deer, how could they not see us?"

Inisha's explanation did little to clear things up and Aranya's attempt to help didn't help much so they tried again to explain how they did it... Finally, the young male simply said, *"As you saw, neither we nor they*  *went anywhere, they just could not see us. We disappeared to them."*

Finally, Justin, Sary's husband spoke up. "I think I see what you are saying… it's like a noise cancelling headphone."   When the large fellow looked at him curiously, he continued while thinking carefully about what he was saying. "With that type of headphone, extra noise is picked up and the signal is amplified, the phase reversed and the result is played back at precisely the same volume as was incoming.   The result is that the incoming signal is exactly matched by a tone of the opposite phase, but a twin in all other ways. The effect is that one cancels he other and the net result is that there is no sound that gets to the ear."

"Yes," Inisha responded enthusiastically, *"That is exactly how it works, I think."*

The discussion carried on for all the hours needed to reach the outlet where Patit Creek met the townsite of Dayton.   The twelve towers of the storage facility was immediately visible on entry to the townsite and, as expected, the tin structures were gone but the silos were there.

Ash lay deeply everywhere… so deep that it was nearly impossible to tell what was here before it fell. In fact, with the exception of the few structures that still rose above the ash, one would never know a thriving town ever existed here. Only the pimples of upthrust mounds of ash served to tell those who knew where the individual buildings of the town once stood.   No search had ever been done of this town.   No one had ever proven that no one had survived. There could be colonies of people left here… but no one knew where they would be.

As soon as the team was on the scene of the grain elevator, the three separate crews moved in to test their individual theories. The plan was to allow each of the three teams to try their plans and gather together at dinner to test which was most efficient and which warranted being actively pursued.

Ronnie Marlowe had remembered that each silo has its own inspection port that allowed the lab crews to gain access to the grain within for necessary testing. In a modern world, nothing was marketed without random testing for quality and purity... so it was with wheat grown in the Palouse country of eastern Washington and western Idaho. Ron simply planned to find these test ports and extract the needed grain. It should be noted that Ronnie's plan worked exactly as planned with one small exception... the only miscalculation centered around how much grain could be readily extracted from the very small access port... it was not much and most fervently hoped that the other methods were able to supply the product at a much faster rate.

Paul Jensen had proposed entering the pit where the trucks dumped and extracting the needed grain from there. He had assured the Committee that he knew how to get from the pit to the silo and thus extract grain. The problem occurred in getting to and into the pit. It was simply buried in many feet of ash and packed tight. The team attempted to excavate enough ash to gain access to the pit, but the going was difficult and the ash packed very tightly. It was very much like trying to excavate a form of concrete.

The third solution had come from Mary Wilson who had worked at the Whetstone Road/Lyons Ferry elevator for many harvests. She knew there would be access to the silo from the top. If her team could scale their way to the very top of the silos where the run gear distributed the incoming grain into individual silos, she was quite sure she could get into the grain stored there.

It took Mary and her team over an hour to find a way to the top of the silos and they did, indeed gain access to the stored grain, but since the level of the grain was well below the access way in at the top, it was felt that getting the grain from the silo to the waiting wagons might prove untenable. There was a ladder that descended to the level of the grain, and much further, it was suspected, but there was no simple way of getting the grain back out. It was suggested that a bucket brigade be formed to hoist it out to where it could be dumped to the waiting crews below for loading. The consensus was that this would work, but would be slow and very labor intensive.

With all three suggestions less than viable, the team got together and brainstormed. One thing that no one had remembered, it seems, is that there are access doors in the sides of the silos low down for access for cleaning when the tubes are empty. Dust accumulation is a major danger for grain storage facilities so cleaning of the towers is extremely important. There have been many instances of such facilities exploding due to the grain dust accumulating and igniting. To preclude that, access and ventilation was of paramount importance to the facilities.

A quick search yielded the fact that large, double doors, did, indeed exist at the base of each tower. The doors were of steel construction and, while they did seem to open outward, they were securely locked and bolted closed.

No one was sure who first mentioned it, but someone suggested that in older elevators like this one, there were doors at regular intervals down the side of the entire length of the tower. Had anyone checked this one for that kind of access? It was a

Silo Doors

quick gasp from Mary that drew the attention of everyone present   "Yes," she said, "there are doors... in the unit I was in, at least at that height, they were on top of the other for the entire range of my vision vertically!"

Quickly, the rather strongly built woman, with a vocabulary to match, called her team together, explained what she had in mind and away they went at a run. It was now just a matter of moments to ascend to the level of the grain in the silo they had entered before. A quick but adequate search revealed the doors she had referenced... openable from the outside and affording access directly into the tons of grain stored there!

A quick, intensive and thorough search turned up the mechanical crank that was used to unlatch the doors in the side of the silo and it was dispatched immediately to the team waiting for it. It had been decided that until people were familiar with the operation of the door, that only the door at the very top of the grain column would be opened.

Since no one had any real idea what would happen if a door were opened that had the pressure of stored grain behind it, it was decided to be safe and cautious for now.

It was a pretty simple matter to open the first door and, as it turned out, the grain level was almost nearly perfectly level with the bottom of the door. Access was pretty simply achieved at that point but sinking in grain to one's waist was not an easy thing to accept for those involved and it made working in the morass very difficult. The first thing the team discovered was that the size of the doorway limited shovelers in the silo to no more than three. There simply was not sufficient room for more to be able to wield their shovels and toss the contents into the passageway. The system works, but it was slow and cumbersome. A chute system was devised that allowed those in the passageway outside the silo to simply shovel the grain into the chute where it descended by gravity to the aperture in the outside wall and freefall to the ground below. A quick inspection revealed that this system was viable as far down the silo as the team needed to descend to meet their needs.

After using this cumbersome method for the first two doors, one wagon was filled and the second about a third full. Mary suggested they move down one level below the level of the grain and open that door. Yes, there would be pressure behind the door, but not that much and it was felt an advantage would be gained. The request brought the expedition leaders to their level on a run and, after the woman explained what they had found in dealing with these doors, it was decided to try what she suggested... in stages.   They excavated the next segment to the middle of the door height then opened the door.

It was surprisingly easy to accomplish. Of course the weight of the grain served to open the door quickly, but not so much that the crew outside could not handle it and prevent the door from slamming open. The grain inside had spilled readily into the passageway, allowing the shovelers there to simply scoop it into the chute and away it went to the waiting wagon below.

Search by idle expedition members had yielded a large roll of heavy duty tarp and someone, seeing this, suggested making a tube of the material and affixing that to the end of the chute. That tarp tube was then lowered to the waiting wagon below and the only shoveling being done now was from the silo into the chute. From there, it descended the canvas tube and loaded directly into the wagon as controlled by the ground team there. It was a pretty ingenious team that devised this solution! But, then, this was a group of people who had lived for over eight years by the ideas they fomented. There was no manual for what they were doing and there was no one to tell them how to do it or that it could not be done. So... they just did it.

Eventually, each door was opened when the grain was at its top. Had they needed more than what they did, they would have opened more than one silo and loaded multiple wagons at a time, but, as it was, by evening, the seven tons of grain wanted had been loaded. Those not allowed to participate in the loading had arranged a comfortable camp and had dinner ready when those who were loading finished. It was a fun and convivial crew gathered around the fire that evening.

No one knew for sure what had made dinner so enjoyable this evening. For sure, watching the sun traverse the evening sky was part of it. Having exceeded their goals for the day was another, but there was an ambiance that exceeded even these important factors.

When dinner was a memory and the aftermath was past, people were sitting and talking... mostly about the future, but eventually the conversation drifted to the events of the day. Sary had been quiet, just letting the conversation go where it would when she remembered the events on the grade. She thought a moment and addressed the two non-human members of their group. "Inisha, what did you do today? I mean, I know you covered our presence so those deer did not know we were there... I watched that happen, but how in the world did you do that?"

At first, there was just that deep, rumbling chuckle when he began to speak in his newly adopted language form... that he had adopted to be able to communicate with their neighbors... though he was not perfect in it, he could speak well enough to be understood. "I cloak us," he said quietly. "I make it so animals not see us. We not go anywhere, we still there, they still there, but they not could see us any more."

The entire assembly was astounded at the words they had just heard. But it was Sary who followed up with the thought. "You mean that you made us invisible while standing there?" As she watched his head nod, she continued, "How did you do that? Is it something I could learn?"

"It is something your people once knew how to do," he retorted. "There is nothing we do that you did not at one time do as well. You could speak directly into another's mind even as I do with you at times. You could cloak yourselves even as I did today. There was nothing we do that you could not do. The problem is, about thirty-five millennia ago, your species stopped adapting to your environment and started adapting your environment to yourselves..."

"Essentially," Ronnie stated, "we moved indoors. We stopped hunting as our primary source of survival and began to add gathering, eventually adding even agriculture to our mix." Turning to Inisha and Aranya, he continued, "I would assume that is the difference between us... we moved indoors and you did not..."

"That very true," the large fellow said. "We remained true to our own creation and retained those things we needed to survive in that creation."

He went on to explain how he had accomplished his amazing feat earlier this day, but that explanation fell well short of understanding in the human community. After several hours of conversation, questions and replies, it was still unclear how this "parlor trick" was accomplished. It was Mary who ventured forth the idea that held sway. "It sounds to me," she stated calmly, "that what you are saying is that what Justin described is actually what happens, but in the right range... is this true?"

"I do not know of this device," the big, hairy fellow stated, "but it sounds to be right. That is done in the visible energy spectrum so the light the thing watching us wants to see does not reach him. It is very effective for us. I don't know if you can do it or not, but I know you once could."

"Wow," the girl shouted, "that is absolutely amazing to me. Yes, there are times it would be so helpful to be able to do this. Right now, however, we have work to consider. I am so glad you finished loading our wheat wagons."

Mary was quiet a moment then spoke, "Sary, do you think the loaded wagons should start back in the morning or do you feel we should all travel together as we came out?"

"I've been considering that, Mary," Sary replied, "and I think we should stick together. If something should happen to a loaded wagon on the way back, the seven would be stranded there until the rest of the brigade arrived later in the day. We may need more help here getting the seed, if we can find any, from that building and I would feel a lot better if the entire brigade traveled together all the way back."

"So, that's how we'll do it then," Mary said with a smile for the woman.

Sunrise found a camp that had been fed a hearty breakfast ready to begin a difficult day. The structure that housed the Farmer's Co-op was down. It had been crushed by the weight of the ash and was buried to a depth yet to be determined, but that was considered to be deep! All the hand tools thought to be needed in this excavation were already loaded into one of the gear designated wagons and

243

driven to the site along with the remaining three empty wagons.

A war council was convened on the spot to decide the best way to attack this obstacle. The warehouse where all the seed stock had been located was identified and the area probed. This building, it seems, was not so badly crushed as was the main showroom of the facility. It was thought that, perhaps, sacks of seed grains were the reason for that. It was theorized that the roof had crushed down to the level of the stacks of palletized sacks and the destruction abated at that point... at least, it was highly hoped it had abated.

Luckily Juan and Manuel Mendoza both had made pick-ups at this warehouse often and were able, between them, to draw a very good representation of what the warehouse had looked like before the disaster had struck. They located the main, roll up door as well as the walk in door that was immediately beside the big door. They explained there had been a concrete tarmac completely surrounding the facility that should still be intact. Their recommendation was to manually excavate a tunnel through the ash to the small door. That tunnel could be shored up and, once the door is open, a decision could be made as to the disposition of the ash in front of it. It could be that just a trench to the door that sloped down from the new soil level would be sufficient for their needs.

When the work began, they had marked off a pathway to the warehouse door that was fifteen feet wide and started fifty feet from the building. The plan was to excavate a ramp down that fifty feet that would be eight feet wide at the door and down the estimated twenty five feet of accumulated ash. They had scavenged enough lumber to get started, at least and they felt they could make adjustments as they proceeded. There was nothing about this written in stone... it would just be determined by what happened along the way. It might become necessary to excavate to a width of fifty feet and back the start up to a hundred feet... no one knew yet what would be coming. How stable was the ash? Would it hold for the shoring or would it just filter through like sand? These were questions to answer as they dug.

In fact, it turned out that the ash was almost like concrete behind the shoring. It did not filter through at all so when the trench had reached a depth of twelve feet, the miners added overhead beams that ran across the tunnel and put boards atop those. In essence, the team was digging a roofed tunnel into the old warehouse at this point. A bottom stringer was laid in in ten foot lengths on each side of the tunnel and vertical risers were installed every five feet. These risers were eight feet long and a second stringer was laid on top of the risers... the risers were nailed to the stringers and no two stringers were allowed to end at the same place. Above the stringers, two inch thick by ten inch wide boards the length the tunnel was wide plus the stringers were placed to form a solid ceiling. Initially, there was room between the top of this roof and the excavated ash above, but slowly the ash slumped to fill this void. The side slope of the trench was stopped at this point and it was maintained vertical from then on. Two by sixes were also added to the outside of the risers on both sides to act as sort of a wall. The team used three two by sixes on each side and prayed that would be sufficient to hold back any ash that might want to fall into the open tunnel area. The addition of the three levels of walls between the upper and lower stringers, in fact, held very well and the team changed positions often so that there were always fresh diggers in the tunnel.

It was debated as to whether to use a floor as well. The fifty percent slope of the tunnel was, indeed, steep, but it was not harsh. People had no trouble negotiating the pathway from the end of the tunnel to the outside world. Up and down the workers went, pushing wheelbarrow loads of ash from within the tunnel... it was soon learned that a couple of people with lines secured to the front of the wheelbarrow and pulling the wheelbarrow out was far more effective than was trying to add more people pushing. It didn't take long before the rigging crew could pull a full wheelbarrow out of the tunnel, dump it... wheel it back in, switch the lines over to the next one before it had been filled completely... in fact it became a matter of pride that the riggers beat the shovelers every time and a contest ensued that added interest and prizes to the work of the day.

By mid-morning, the tunnel was at the warehouse. The walk in door had been located and cleared and the team was wondering how to defeat the lock that was keeping the door firmly closed against the best efforts of the team. After several attempts at cajoling the lock open without success, Billy Simmons came up with the solution. Walking into the tunnel with a ten pound sledgehammer, he dismissed all those around him and proceeded to test his room a bit with a practice swing or two before wailing back with a mighty flail and smacking the doorknob dead on and bending it downward at an angle exceeding sixty degrees. One more mighty swing and it simply popped off the door and bounced around on the ash of the floor.

Before he could reach in with a screwdriver to flip back the latch, a shout of "Hold it!" rang out, stopping him in mid thrust. The voice continued, "That has been closed up for eight and a half years. We have no idea if that air is good or stale or deadly! Some toxic chemical may have been broken and spilled in there in the ensuing years. We have oxygen here and I think we should use it."

Billy, with his oxygen mask in place and attached to small oxygen bottle rescued some years before, but still viable, worked his magic on the broken door latch and it was just the work of moments until the door swung outwardly on its own followed by several hundred pounds of ash that had been held in place by the door. To himself, Billy thought about the futility of wearing oxygen only to find the back side of the door as packed with ash was the front side had been.

The excavators were called back in but if turned out to only be a short time as this was evidently a large drift that had blown in against the door. As soon as they broke through, the crew was called out and Billy reentered with his oxygen system to do a bit of exploration.

The first order of business was opening the aperture further to allow more light into the interior and to get some fresh air into the space. The flame on his carbide lamp was burning very low, telling him of the low level of oxygen in the atmosphere of the interior... as soon as he had cleared a substantial hole in the drifted ash, his little light glowed just a bit brighter, affording him the ability to get a look at the interior of the warehouse. His first look was up to the roof where what he saw did not fill him with any great degree of confidence. The roof was crushed... he felt very much like he was on the inside of a crushed beer can, looking out.

He was surprised to see large stacks of paper sacks of something stacked to the roof. It was obviously this unexpected support that kept the roof from collapsing totally. The problem now was that with the roof resting on the top of the stack, what was going to happen if parts were removed from below. Billy waited a few minutes until his eyes had adjusted as much as they were going to do before he began his search in earnest. As he expected, the large stacks that had helped keep the roof up were, in fact, seed stock... the difference was, it was not the grass seed he had expected but was seed peas. When the young man saw this, the remembered that on the slopes of the Blue Mountains, many of the wheat growers grew a strip of peas along the outside of the wheat. These sacks would probably be of great importance later, but as of right now, they could serve best in the exact spot where they now resided.

In answer to a hail from outside, Bill suggested that they allow a few more minutes of air exchange before entering the tight building. He did retreat to a spot nearer the door to explain what he had found and the good news that further excavation was probably not going to be necessary at this time. While this was good news to the shovel crew, the wagon crews began to become more anxious, knowing they would soon be front and center in this effort.

A few minutes later, Sary entered the dark room with a lantern fueled by the most precious of carefully horded fuel. Amazingly, however, her one lantern lit up the entire space brightly. Immediately, the two people began a search of the space. One stack contained about two tons of alfalfa seed while another had about five tons of a pasture grass mix. This was a fine combination as the two would grow well together and provide superior pasture for the stock the colony now had and would have for quite some time to come.

A pleasant surprise came when one whole side of the warehouse was found to contain corn seed. There were various other seeds available here as well... and all were valuable to the colony. While digging in a secluded spot, sacks of milo seed showed up and behind that commodity was a large area filled with all sorts of hand tools. There were shovels and rakes. Next to them were axes and mattocks. Even further along were peaveys and other log and lumber handling tools. The explorers found a veritable treasure trove of the things they needed most to carry on in their life in the style to which they were now constrained to live.

Vegetable seeds of all kinds were found by the case. Even fruit tree seeds were there although it was so rare to rear them from a seed as most were adventitiously seeded or cut from fruit stock.

By midday, the remaining wagons were full to the gunwales with precious seed and even more precious implements and tools. There were even some carpentry tools and metal working tools available there. Everyone was now extremely curious as to what the main showroom would house, but there was no time now, nor was there wagon room to load it had there been time. It was a simple trip to return to this spot at any time to finish what they had started. "Besides," Sary stated matter-of-factly, "it's not like someone else is apt to show up and take it before we return... and if they do, they have to need it a dearly!"

It was a happy and boisterous crew that Sary returned with into their valley home. The people that came out to meet them wondered at their great good mood. It was obvious that they had succeeded at their task... what was less obvious was how much they had exceeded the expectations they carried with them. When the news of what the crews had returned to the colony spread, people came in from their stakes to share in the celebration and to congratulate the young woman, Sary, on the success of her first "command" task.

Chapter 18
The Work Begins

Sunshine... oh how blessed it was to awake in the morning and see it peeking over the eastern rim to light the valley. There was not a person in the colony but who felt rejuvenated and renewed by the sight of actual, unfiltered sunlight greeting them.

These people knew that this could only be temporary. After the warehouse in Dayton had been salvaged clear, an expedition was mounted to the Walla Walla area to see if similar results could be achieved. The expedition, as it crossed the promontory that led down into the basin where the city had once resided, could see far to the southwest and it was obvious that there were still volcanoes erupting in the Cascade Mountains further to the south. How many and how severely could not be judged, but there were many options available. Mt. Jefferson, The Three Sisters, Mt. Washington, Mt. Mazama and Mt. McLaughlin were but a few of those Cascade peaks that had been in full eruption. How many continued now, no one knew, but it was obvious that all was not done yet. While not as outrageously successful as the Dayton expedition, several tons of usable seed and supplies were rescued from the Farm Co-op there and, even more importantly, many horse drawn farm implements were retrieved from the museum there. Many would need restoration, especially of the wooden components, before they could be used, but with thousands of square miles of dead timber easily at hand, that was not deemed to be a major factor. One of the more immediately usable devices located was a complete smithy. Forge, anvil, bellows... even sacks of coal as well as all the tongs, hammers, punches and other hand tools were there for them. This set up would be most helpful in getting the colony farm up and operating. One sure thing about machinery... sooner or later it would break down!

In the valley, changes were underway. Thousands of acres had been seeded to prevent blowing ash by the summer winds from making things totally miserable. The serendipity of this was that there were now many acres of fresh pasture land for the colony's growing animal populations. Rabbits, while tasty enough and certainly healthy enough became rather routine fare after over eight years of living on them virtually alone. Now, the herds of cattle could be expanded and within a few years, would even begin to contribute to the overall food bank of the group. Today, however, expanding the herd was of highest importance with only the occasional cull being removed and butchered.

While a great deal of grains like corn had been being grown inside the barns, large quantities were not possible due to the competition for available space. Priorities had to be assigned for the use of the entire colony and limited space was allocated to corn production. With the cessation of ashfall, there were no restrictions on what could be grown out of doors.

A meeting of the Committee of the Whole produced a Colonial Charter which was presented to the colony as a whole and was ratified on the first vote... though not without debate on many facets thereof. This Charter called for Communal living for the next ten years at which time, the issue would be reviewed and a new vote taken. At that time, the system could be extended or abolished however the colony decided.

It was a rather impassioned lecture by Rae Lynn Stuart on the success and failures of the "United Order" as lived by the early Mormon pioneers in their settlement of the valleys in the Great Basin in the middle nineteenth century that led to this stepped in structure of their colonial government. The woman explained that the system, much the same as what the colony was now living under worked well for short periods during the establishment and early growth of the various settlements set out by Brigham Young and his Brethren.

Under the auspices of the Church, these small colonies moved into a remote but arable valley to establish a new community. For some time, until the community was viable and self-supporting, it lived under what the Church Leaders had named the "United Order". In essence, it was the purest form of socialism. All members of society worked for the common good of the entire society. All food was grown and stored and kept in trust for the entire community. Each individual family drew from this common store as needed for their own needs. They were, in the purest sense, a commune. The system worked very well initially, but with time and prosperity, it waned. Subsequent study showed the fatal flaw in the system quite plainly... as long as there was a sense of extreme need, the plan was flawless. People did their level best to produce at the highest possible levels. No one wished to return to the Salt Lake Valley a failure, so these communities survived and prospered. They were evident all over the Great Basin right up until the time of the great calamity. Communities such as Logan, Utah and Blackfoot, Idaho... Preston, Idaho and Evanston, Wyoming all owed their very existence to this system.

In each and every case, the Church Leaders had sent out a well-equipped colony to settle these valleys and to create a living, working, breathing community therein who looked to the Church in Salt Lake Basin for guidance and leadership. The entire area was settled in just this way and it worked well... until the community began to prosper.

With prosperity came greed. While times were hard and survival not assured, the community very carefully worked together to assure survival, but when there began to be surplus, there was always someone there wanting more than what they actually needed to make do. When the causes were identified and those identified who took this path, it was found, almost universally, to be mothers who were guilty of the excesses. While the results of investigation, at first, seemed surprising, a bit of thought showed the underlying flaw. It was not for themselves that these good women wanted more, but for their children! The women were more than willing to limit their own whims and wishes to the standard of the community, but when it came to their children, they wanted more! It was the children who were, then, the cause of the end of the United Order.

Rae Lynn made sure everyone present at the meeting understood the dangers of the plan and the need for limiting the term thereof. It was in special session following the insightful woman's discourse that the Committee decided on the ten year plan. When all understood the rationale behind this term, it was the matter of but a single vote for the entire package to carry by an extremely wide margin.

There were very few founding families who had not selected their stake acreage and most were making more definite plans to move onto their own ground "soon"... even after the stake farms were delineated, there were huge blocks of unclaimed ground that remained under the auspices of the Committee. It was essential that these lands be seeded as well as the stake acres, so a committee was appointed to decide the best use of these grounds and to decide how to effect that use. The committee was given two weeks to have a working plan for the community lands.

As a result, the committee formulated a set of concepts, rules and regulations to manage the public lands. These ideas where hammered out in private session then brought up, discussed, modified, accepted or rejected item by item until a consensus was reached.

It was decided that to these large plots the irrigation waters would be brought. Anyone who wanted irrigation on their own stake acres could either continue the system from here to their own ground, or could tap their own source... which in most cases meant the river itself since most stake acres were along the main river. It was decided as part of the committee's work that a "Water Commission" would be established with the authority to regulate the private use of the public water resource. Although there was some grumbling about "Big Brother", most agreed that water was too important a commodity to be left unprotected. Since almost all land had to be irrigated strictly by flooding, careful planning was necessary to make sure gravity would do the job sufficiently.

Probably the biggest draw on the labor force began immediately after the planting was complete. Although the valley had accumulated far less ashfall than had the open prairies outside the valley, there was still over fifteen feet of ash everywhere in the valley. The consensus was that in the fields it would just become part of the home soil, but around the buildings, it was dangerous at worst, but an inconvenience at best. It had long been desired that access to the buildings that survived be improved by the removal of the mountains of ash up against them and on top of them. It was felt that the absence of rain had been instrumental in the saving of the buildings they were using, but that was not something that could be relied on for long.

The decision was made and resources allocated to clear the ash from all buildings in use for any of the colony's purposes. Volunteers were called for and work gangs assigned and the task began. The large scoop shovels rescued from the Co-op stores were a huge help in this task. It was amazing how many wagon loads it took to clear each building but they persevered! Within the month, every community building was uncovered.

The summer was as close to idyllic as anything these people had known for eight years. Everything was seeded that could be seeded. Water was flowing to the fields. Corn was growing, the pastures were all green and enough ash had been removed from the buildings to make access and egress much simpler than at any time in the past.

Jenna had noticed that she was seeing Inisha quite regularly, but she had not seen anything of Aranya in some days. One evening in the barn as they were finishing up the day, she asked the big guy, "Where is Aranya? I haven't seen her for days and I miss her."

The large, hairy guy looked at the woman and stated, as you know we can't do our meetings so it is past the time she should have a mate. We have found a male who needs a mate and she has gone to meet him. He lives almost to the great ocean in the east, but if they decide to do this thing, they will return here after mating there. It is how we do such things."

"Why are you not yet mated, my friend?" the girl asked the big fellow. "I know you are older than most of your people who mate for the first time."

"It is past time, but with all that has happened, it is not possible now," the big guy said. "Our custom is for the male to go to the clan of the female and our clan cannot spare me just now. We lost too many of our males that

night. It is costly to the home clan to lose a female too, so the few we have found who have mateable age females are reluctant to let them leave. So, I am stuck between for now. Everywhere our population has been hard hit by this event... many places even more than we were here. We will wait to see what happens. I hold out hope that something can be worked out soon. Having the food supplies we have here is a huge help. So many of our people did not have such a thing and many were lost."

"How badly was your group hit?" the young woman asked.

Inisha was quiet for a moment then answered deliberately, "Before, we numbered eighteen in our clan and we one of three clans that claimed these mountains as our home. Today, we are the only clan remaining and we are reduced to eight members only."

Shock was the first thing Jenna felt as she thought about this. In an area of over nine thousand square miles, when times were good, there were less than sixty of these people populating it. And today there were but eight! As she contemplated this, she began to realize just how tenuous their survival was. She asked, "How many more of you have you found?"

Inisha was very quiet for just a bit then, very solemnly, he answered, "We cannot identify more than two hundred individuals living in all of North America. I am sure there are others that we have not yet located, but that is all we have established contact with across this land."

After a short pause, the young man continued. "Kenora, my sire, has arranged for a conference of those clan leaders with whom we have contact. He has an idea to put forth to the surviving clans that may help us. He has not told me exactly what it is he is going to propose, but, I think it might have to do with combining some clans and moving other clans closer. This should happen soon... within the next few days, we hope and then we may have some changes to make. We have a wonderful situation here, but we are not anxious to bring more into it because it may mean more problems for you with a larger population of us to feed and care for."

"Do not let that aspect bother you," the girl replied. "We are doing what we are doing here for your people. We have found you at last. We have no desire to lose you now! You are not difficult to maintain. You eat little, surprisingly little for your size so your people have not strained our ability to produce sufficient for your needs. As you know, we, the entire colony, set this area aside for just your use. Our goal here is to maintain you and sustain you in  whatever way works best for you. We who live on this ranch do so to serve your people."

She continued. "You have taught us so much that we needed so desperately. Your knowledge of herbal and natural medicines as well as your energy applications have been more than valuable in the treatment of illnesses of my people. Believe me, our doctors have been amazed by what you have been able to accomplish with the methods you employ. It is true that I am but one person here in a community of a few hundred, but I am very safe in saying that whatever the four of us on this ranch recommend as pertains to you and your group will be allowed by the community as a whole."

After a short pause to contemplate, she continued. "I recommend you tell Kenora just what I have said and I will bring up your plight to my people. We will decide this together and we will do what is best for all concerned... fair deal?

"That sounds exceedingly fair, Little Miss," the large, dark fellow replied as he grinned. "This has been a sudden discussion but it is fruitful, I think. I thought you would feel this way as well as Kayla and your mates. I was less sure about the rest of the colony. We will proceed on this understanding for now then if that is proper."

"That is totally proper," the woman replied as her oldest son climbed up on her lap to get closer to the large, hairy fellow he loved so much.

Chapter 19
In the Way of Life

The December sun rose late and did not rise high over the colony at the River, but it rose over a jubilant group of people as they had gathered to kick of a celebration of the twenty-five years that had elapsed since the mud stopped falling from the skies. No one, it turned out wanted to measure new time from the tragedy of the impact, but all were unanimous in choosing the end of fall as the spark of the new calendar. The time before had little meaning now... and few remembered it anymore.

Jared was not as spry as he once had been... years and years of hard labor has a way of slowing us down sooner than we'd like, but the earliest leader of this group had four tall, strong sons standing with him, three with sons of their own and the last soon to be wed. Three daughters of the soil stood beside  their brothers and made the man know that he was expected to sit at the front and accept his rightful due from those assembled. For, this celebration, the Silver Anniversary of life on the prairie was a tribute to those who held it all together in the light of those earliest times.

Saving seed

Some were gone now... Colonel Kline... Lila Baylor... Dr. Kyle... too many gone too young but the survivors were strong now.

The food warehouses were full with the end of harvest in the year 25. Fields were being planted to crops other than food now as the labor became available. Cotton,

Flood Irrigate

flax and sisal were being grown and harvested for the products that could be made from them. A whole new industry arose from these plants and the heavy cloth made from the coarse cotton and wool shorn from their own flock made for strong work clothes.

It was such a calamity to engineer and build a workable loom to weave their thread with may starts and stops, redesigns and tests. Trial and error were the words of the day on that project as well as many others. It took some time, but it worked and soon there were people volunteering to learn the process to make the cloth the colony needed.

The population had increased significantly in these years. Most was due to the huge increase in birth rate among the colonists that began with the organization at the old place in "town". The response to the call for controlled parenting so as to maintain genetic parity was well received and led to a "baby boom" of a large magnitude. Today, the population had returned to more logical increase without the pressure of need to give so prevalent within. The interesting fact was, the colony was very heavy with those under twenty-five years of age with the huge anomaly of a very low number of twenty-five to thirty-five year olds and a more normal split of those above thirty-five until the oldest were counted. Once again, their numbers decreased rapidly, with only a very few of the very old remaining.

The diseases of the early days were very hard on the very young and the very old and the stress of returning to hard labor after a lifetime of office work took its toll as well.

There had been some influx as well as the occasional straggler or two or five found their way to the colony. Bart and Will kept their earth station radios up and running day and night to monitor for traffic. Both were well advanced in years, though to look at Bart's family would never guess this to be true. Stella had given him seven children before she decided that they had done their part for the survival of the species. Four sons and three daughters made Bart's life easy to live. Further, it allowed him time to pursue his passion that was his radio.

Between he and Will, they had located only three other pockets of population in all of North America... and all of those to the south. It had been pretty much decided that the impact had occurred in the Hudson's Bay region of Canada and the effects were such that survival had been impossible. They had found one center in Peru, but the population was too small and they could not maintain genetic purity. No one gave this group any chance of maturing.

The rest of South America was dead. There were not radio broadcasts to be heard from anywhere there. As long as they had their Peru contact they would keep using him, but no one held out very much hope.

The contact they had in Mexico was strong. They were in stronghold in a mountain valley near Lake Chapala, not that far from Mexico City… a place of over twenty-two-million people who were snuffed out in virtually one night. The little colony was doing well because, as with this one, it was a community of the same church that had saved this group. They were used to hard work and were able 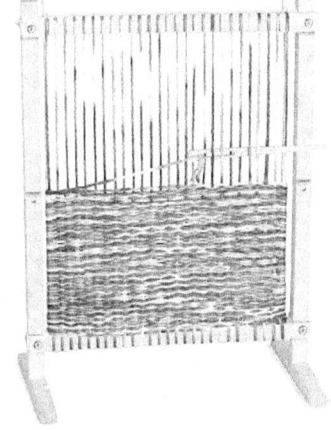 to survive the ashfall on what was stored and to begin to thrive in the return of the sun.

The last one in North America was in the southeast. It seemed to be loud and boisterous now, though they told of the same hard times that beset the northwestern group. They were also a young and lively group and all looked good for them now. They had sent out search patrols that had ridden all the way to Virginia and found nothing except the occasional small band of desperate people running from the north. The word they carried was not pleasant and eventually caused the cessation of their explorations.

War was the word from the north and northeast of the country. Those few of the millions who had lived there who survived the initial blast had formed armies to try to protect themselves. Their armies were beset by armies formed by the criminal element and, since these had been law-abiding  people and followed the strict gun control policies in effect at the time of the calamity in the eastern states, were virtually unarmed while facing thugs with fully automatic weapons. It did not take rocket science to figure what was going down in those concrete jungles. It was, in essence the same as what happened with the little area in southeastern Washington... the thugs could not survive when there were no more victims to be robbed.

The last station they knew of was in Arizona and the news from there was the same... they were a small group and might not survive if they couldn't widen their gene pool, but they were fed now and they were surviving, there were just too few of them.

They had sent out parties looking for others to incorporate, but as they got further west, the same thing that plagued the Midwest had hit here as well... with the impact

Sary & Justin's Daughter, Sky takes Adam and Rae Lyn's son Landis to Wed

came the volcanic eruptions throughout the Sierra Nevada range and that had cause major slippage of the tectonic plates resulting in major earthquakes all along the San Andreas and other fault lines from Mexico to Canada. This did not bode well for the coastal areas as was being evidenced.

The sasquatch people on the ranch were thriving. Eventually, most of those in the western region had been called to their preserve to start over again. There were twenty-three adults now living in the preserve and that ranch was providing food to more population centers across all of North America. In addition, the ranch was supplying some meat to the River Colony as well.

As evening approached, the people gathered at the main pavilion that had been erected at the mouth of the Tucannon River Canyon. It had been a wonderful day of good-hearted play and remembrance as the Colony

Waiting for fun to start

celebrated their deliverance from the Hell of that eight years of ash fall. Jenna DeWitt was the chair for the night's entertainment and her daughter, Angela, was the featured singer. Grampa DeWitt had been recruited to ride herd on Angela's more than lively pair.

All the children in the Colony we a bit overindulged and these two were no exception. Add that to their natural precocity and it was easy to see why they were such a handful for any one person. Grampa always seemed to have the best chance with them, so he was once again called on to work his magic!

Jenna was within minutes of taking the stage to set the evening in motion when a cry called out into the gloaming from one of the continuously manned watch towers erected at the access points to the canyon.

Instantly, the defense force was in action. A squad of well-armed militiamen had moved into a strong defensive position even as reports from the redoubt were coming in on the nature of the threat... three wagons were approaching from the east… not as new as some that had come, but better than others, for sure. A strong squad mounted and rode out to greet them before they got anywhere near the population center… to meet and stop them there so their intent could be learned before injury could result. This was assuredly a lesson learned the hard way and that was a short-lived mistake that would never again be allowed to happen.

Drew Johnston rode at the head of the squad and, as they neared their objective, he directed them to spread out, half surrounding the wagons in a semi-circle ahead of and in the line of their travel. It was a sorry lot of people he was looking at here. There were ten of them in all above the age of fourteen or so. It appeared there were six adults and four adolescents in the group, two male and two female. In addition there were another five younger children down to the age of six or so. There did not appear to be any very young… a pretty common situation with the refugee groups they now encountered. While it was true life was easier since the cessation of ash fall, it was still no assured thing.

A quick interview told Drew, and those listening that this was a group from the panhandle of Idaho. They had managed to get through so far, but this was all that was left of them and they knew they could not survive in such a small group, so set out to see if they could find others like themselves. Until today, they had seen no one. It was, they said, like traveling earth before man was invented. Only rarely were even the trappings of man encountered… the occasional grain elevator still standing or perhaps a Quonset full of spuds or some other commodity. It was these that kept them alive and living… not necessarily the same thing.

After a careful interview, and a search of their backtrail in the ensuing days, the group was told they were welcome to join the Colony if they would agree to the rules and structure as it was set up. That they were now over eight hundred people put them well within the range of a viable colony and the only thing that threatened them was the spectre of discord from time to time. To attempt to counteract that effect, an ombudsman was appointed whose sole purpose was to arbitrate disagreements impartially.

It was evident that not all such disputes would be settled to the pleasure of all involved, an appeal process was instituted, first to a panel of seven, then to a panel of twenty-one, and finally to the group as a whole. If one side or the other of such a dispute carried it that far, a referendum of the whole would be held and, after both sides of the dispute carefully explained, a vote was cast and a tally taken. As always, the loser in that effort was allowed the option of remaining and accepting the will of the Colony or of taking his chances on his own. If he held Stake Acreage, he would be supplied with food and supplies as compensation for what he was leaving and he was free to leave.

Over the past twenty-five years, a few had left. Most only moved a few miles away to the better farmsteads along the Snake River in the vicinity. Most remained loosely connected to the Colony, even serving as an early warning system for the greater Colony. These separatists went no farther from the Colony than could be covered quickly in case of attack or calamity. In most cases, there was no enmity between factions, even those who chose to leave and the population of the Colony... but they did understand that their needs were left on the back burner until all of the

Colony's needs were addressed and sufficient put by for all in the valley. There had never been a case of capital stature but there had been expulsions. These seemed to have calmed and returned to a civil basis within a short period of time.

All this was well and good, but tonight was a night of celebration… a quarter century of independence and a new tomorrow and tonight there were new people to meet and greet… to get settled and explain the parameters of life in the Colony… of life under the new order… of life After Armageddon…